GOING TO CHURCH

A user's guide

John Pritchard

For Ruth Etchells,
encourager, friend and inspiration

First published in Great Britain in 2009

Society for Promoting Christian Knowledge
36 Causton Street
London SW1P 4ST

The author and publisher have made every effort to ensure that the external website and email addresses included in this book are correct and up to date at the time of going to press. The author and publisher are not responsible for the content, quality or continuing accessibility of the sites.

Unless otherwise noted, Scripture quotations are taken from the New Revised Standard Version of the Bible, Anglicized Edition, copyright © 1989, 1995 by the Division of Christian Education of the National Council of the Churches of Christ in the USA. Used by permission. All rights reserved.

British Library Cataloguing-in-Publication Data
A catalogue record for this book is available from the British Library

ISBN 978–0–281–05810–5

1 3 5 7 9 10 8 6 4 2

Typeset by Kenneth Burnley, Wirral, Cheshire
Printed in Great Britain by Ashford Colour Press

Produced on paper from sustainable forests

Contents

⇒➤●◄⇐

About the author		iv
Introduction: Why write this book?		v

Part 1: The Church as it is

1	Reasons for not going to church	2
2	Why is going to church worth it?	9
3	So you're going (back) to church	15
4	Star ratings	21
5	Vicars – all shapes and sizes	25
6	Ten things to do in a boring sermon	29
7	'The cold smell of sacred stone'	33
8	Putting the Church on a larger map	38
9	Ten things you never hear said in church	41

Part 2: The Church as it should be

10	Q: What's the Church for? A: Worship	44
11	Q: What's the Church for? A: Mission	50
12	Q: What's the Church for? A: Community	58
13	Q: What's the Church for? A: Restoring the sacred centre	66
14	Images of the Church	74
15	Mind the gap	79
16	My kind of church	84
17	Making the most of the service	92
18	Ten things the Church is not	99

Part 3: The Church as it might become

19	The Church of the future	104
20	Ten things to go to the stake for	113
21	So, why go to church?	118
Notes		119

About the author

John Pritchard is Bishop of Oxford and was formerly Bishop of Jarrow. He was Archdeacon of Canterbury and, before that, Warden of Cranmer Hall, Durham. He has served in parishes in Birmingham and Taunton, and has been Diocesan Youth Officer for Bath and Wells diocese. Other books by the author include *The Intercessions Handbook*, *The Second Intercessions Handbook*, *Beginning Again*, *How to Pray*, *Living Easter through the Year*, *How to Explain Your Faith* and *The Life and Work of a Priest*. He is married to Wendy and has two married daughters.

Introduction: Why write this book?

I suppose the answer goes back a few years. I began to realize how wide the gulf had become between those who regard going to church as a perfectly normal, healthy activity, and those who see it as a bizarre survival of a superstitious age, when I read a Sunday newspaper article by a feature writer who had recently attended a baptism. He was aghast at what he saw as a frightening cultic ritual from which he was desperate to escape. It made no sense to him whatever.

> A ritual is being organised, quite a frightening one, with people standing in formation around the central focal point, the . . . altar, and, my God! Someone's carrying a *baby* towards them! My tabloid-conditioned satanic abuse needle gives a jolt. The priest says 'Are you willing to teach her by your prayers?' And the parents of the baby chant: 'We are.' Then they all chant: 'Protect her from evil . . . fill her with your Holy Spirit.' The priest says: 'Do you turn to Christ?' They chant: 'I turn to Christ.' 'Do you repent of your sins?' 'I repent of my sins.' 'Do you renounce evil?' 'I renounce evil.' I can't believe this: I'm cringing, I want to escape. What have I got mixed up in here? These people, like druids round a campfire, warding off evil spirits . . . And they really said it: '*I renounce evil.*'[1]

There's something deeply worrying here – an almost total incomprehension about the nature of ritual and the reality of good and evil, but it also reveals the gulf between conventional religious practice and some sections of contemporary Western society.

Other commentators are only a little kinder. Mary Ann Sieghart, writing in *The Times* one Easter, wrote:

If the Church of England were a car, what sort of car would it be? Maybe an [M-reg] Ford Sierra estate, once white but now slightly battered and grey, smelling a bit musty inside, the sort of car that picks you up from the taxi queue at a country station. It functions perfectly well, and still has years of life in it, but you would not want to rely on it in a blizzard, and you find it faintly embarrassing to drive.[2]

The problem of going to church isn't all in the eyes of newspaper columnists either. Some of it emerges much closer to home. There's an old story that makes the point. It was Sunday morning and a mother went to wake up her son. 'Come on now,' she said, 'time to get up and go to church.' The son moaned loudly. 'I don't want to go to church,' he said. 'Come on,' she coaxed soothingly, 'you know we go to church on Sunday morning.' 'Why should I?' he said. 'They don't like me and I don't like them.' 'Well – two reasons,' said his mother; 'first, you're 42 years old, and second, you're the vicar!'

Sometimes even regular churchgoers wonder if there isn't something more enjoyable to do than struggle out of bed, organize the children, get the lunch on, drive to church, and then sit through 80 minutes of substandard worship full of minor irritations, only to emerge frazzled and frustrated after weak coffee and soft biscuits, having lost one child and nearly lost one's temper. Wouldn't it be easier to be a contented non-believer? Wouldn't a lie-in, brunch and the Sunday newspapers be a better preparation for the coming week?

My role as a Bishop allows me to experience all kinds of worship, and usually a bit of extra effort has gone into it. And I'm fortunate – I move on every week! Sometimes I can barely see out of the chancel, so dense is the incense. Next week I might be at a café-church where we're sitting around tables and I'm not sure whether the service has started. Then again, I can enjoy the dignified theatre of a cathedral Eucharist, or the cold shock of an outdoor baptism. When in Africa I've experienced the contagious, rhythmic singing and dancing of the Mothers' Union, and in Russia, the close harmonies and deep, dark voices of the Orthodox liturgy. I've presided at Communion by a quiet lake in the Quantock hills, in the magical old church at Taizé, and week by week with the people I loved and served in a parish in Taunton.

I've been lucky. But what about those who have a local church that

Regular worshippers were upgraded to first class.

strains the bonds of loyalty and makes the bottle of wine at lunchtime especially welcome? What about the person who feels drawn to the mystery of something deeper in life, but is faced with the banality of an under-cooked 'Family Service'? What about the family, hesitatingly appearing in church for the first time, finding themselves frozen out by a church full of cliques? There are questions to answer. Indeed, one main one: Why go to church?

This is a book for people wondering whether to keep going to church and for those who are wondering whether to try it. These days going to church is much more a decision than a convention. I want to argue that it's worth it. I want to be honest about the problems but confident about the value. The local church is one of God's shop windows. Not his only one – the glories of nature and the beauty of the arts are other striking windows onto God's nature. But if we are interested in the possibility of faith then the local church is a vital place to go to. And if we have been going for a long time and are increasingly wondering why, I hope this book may be an encouragement to stick in there. The stakes are high.

In this book I'm trying, in a fairly random way, to offer a number of answers to the question 'Why go to church?' I don't want to underestimate the difficulties and so I attempt to stand with the sceptics as well as the faithful. But whenever I identify the problems, I hope it will be seen that I do so affectionately. I love the Church, which has brought me great pleasure, deep friendships, much intellectual stimulation and above all, the huge privilege of knowing God. The Church is the family of God's people, an extraordinary body of saints and sinners, a place of nurture, discovery, exploration, wonder, gratitude and service. It's the best that God has to offer. The Orthodox say the Church is life, light and truth. If it isn't, the fault is ours.

There are three sections in the book – the first looking at the Church as it is, the second at the Church as it's meant to be, and the third at the Church as it might become. I hope they might inspire us all to re-engage with this lovely but wounded Bride of Christ, offering our gifts and experience to prepare her more fully for her wedding day.

Changing the image, I'd like this book to be a route-finder through the mess, mystery and magic of the Church, giving the reader more understanding and more hope. I trust we might catch a vision of the Church as a flawed but wonderful band of pilgrims, worshipping, serving and having fun in the light of God's love.

My thanks as ever go to the noble band who keep me on the road when I'm writing – my wife Wendy, secretaries Christine Lodge and Debbie Perry, Amanda Bloor my chaplain, and Whitby the cat, whose exploits in living by faith when up a tree are yet to be told. Some people gallantly read the manuscript and, particularly in Wendy's case, mercilessly revealed its weaknesses. Alison Barr, my editor, serenely oversaw the whole process and has my warm thanks. As does Ron Wood whose wonderful, wry cartoons refresh many pages of the book.

I believe the healthiest stance we can take in relation to the Church is that of loyal rebels – 'loyal' because this is the Body of Christ himself, who deserves our ultimate commitment, and 'rebels' because we must never be satisfied with the Church until that Body is reunited with the ascended Lord, and all things are brought to fulfilment in him.

We have a long way to go, but be patient – God isn't finished with us yet.

John Pritchard

PART 1

The Church as it is

1

Reasons for not going to church

Until a few years ago, Christians could be a bit smug about people who didn't go to church. They could say it was a bit like not having a wash – the excuses for not doing so were pretty feeble. 'I was made to wash as a child.' 'I just don't have time to wash these days.' 'I used to wash but it got boring so I stopped.' 'I still wash on special occasions like Christmas and Easter.' 'None of my friends wash.' 'People who make soap are only after your money.' 'The bathroom's never warm enough' (I have sympathy with that one).

Now, however, this self-satisfied approach seems outdated and simplistic. There are lots of good reasons for not going to church. Indeed, the boot is on the other foot. Why *would* ordinary, decent, reasonable people disrupt family life on a Sunday morning to attend church? Let's look at the problems. I won't spare the critique – we have to face popular misgivings squarely and honestly. But I don't accept that is all that can be said of course; that's what the rest of the book is about!

'I don't believe in God'

Not believing in God seems pretty rock-solid as a reason for staying in bed on Sunday morning. Worshipping a God you don't believe in would seem to be a curious use of time, on a par with leaving messages in the fireplace for Father Christmas, or looking out for low-flying storks when a baby is due. On the other hand, this reason for not going to church has to be used with care because you just never know . . . there are very good intellectual reasons for believing in God, and it's worth having an honest look. In any case, the passing years have a strange way of reversing your youthful convictions (as in 'It's all down-hill after 40' or 'My parents don't understand a thing'). Sometimes these about-turns are of major proportions. The world-famous philosopher Antony Flew had made quite a name for himself as an outspoken atheist until, in later life, he became convinced of the reality and necessity of God. He believes now that the only good explanation of the origin of life and the complexity of nature is a Supreme Intelligence. It's a 'conversion' that can leave no atheist untroubled.[1]

'The Church is a hierarchical, controlling institution in an age of freedom and choice'

In other words, the Church as a whole is one of those oppressive institutions we began to throw off in the 1960s and whose agonizing demise we've been watching ever since. It's simply not fit for purpose in handling our spiritual needs. Bono of the band U2 once said: 'I'm not into religion. I'm completely anti-religious. Religion is a term for a collection, a denomination. I am interested in personal experience of God.' (Interestingly, Bono has since found churches to be essential partners in his humanitarian campaigns and says, sheepishly: 'I'm starting to like these church people.') To many people the Church controls and restricts human freedom. Its rigidity, both in doctrine and morality, means that it takes up conservative stances on ethical issues and seeks to impose those views on society at large. The Church is out of touch, out of time and out of favour. Why would I join it?

'I used to go, but . . .'

How often does a priest or pastor hear that line? There are still huge numbers of people in our society who used to go to church but stopped when they got to secondary school because nobody else went any more, or they moved house and somehow never got linked up with a new church, or they got caught up in a church row and said they'd never darken the doors again, or they fell out with the vicar, or they were over-worked in church and swore never to get involved again, or they got divorced and felt misunderstood. The reasons are legion. Family life got too complex with all the demands on those precious weekends which turn out to be the only family space left – this is a genuine dilemma. Or maybe the church was too conservative/became too charismatic/gave me no help with my depression, bereavement, unemployment – it goes on. Saddest of all, perhaps, is the charge that someone had honest questions and doubts and couldn't find any way of raising them or having them dealt with in an adult fashion, so that belief became less and less persuasive and he or she drifted into agnosticism.

'I just don't see the point'

Ah! Tricky. Without some touch of the Divine Magician, some intimation of immortality, some whisper from a strange land, it's hard to see what going to church has got, that going out for the day, having a long pub lunch or dozing in the garden hasn't got. You can't manufacture divine longing. In any case, many people find that their spiritual needs are met through climbing mountains or listening to music. On the other hand, a Christian is entitled to wonder whether people always listen closely enough to that whisper in the night, that desire to say 'Thank you', that disturbing shift in the internal landscape. There may be an alternative narrative after all . . .

'The services are dire'

This reason for not going to church is a humdinger. It takes any number of forms, all of which, on a bad day, I have experienced. Hymns are squeezed out of a terminally ill organ or brutally murdered by what used to be called a choir. A contemporary variation is the music group singing fervently but with an Olympian disregard for the embarrassment of the congregation, particularly the men. The readings are utterly obscure, and the prayers are alternately tedious and off-the-wall. The sermon is naïve to the point of parody and shows no awareness of the contemporary world, the subtlety of biblical interpretation, or the fact that Edna Bucket is snoring loudly. Follow this up with what is fondly called 'fellowship over coffee' but which, for the newcomer, is more like an exercise in exclusion, and you have to wonder why people are surprised that their church doesn't grow.

A young woman went to church for the first time since her baptism 20 years before. She said afterwards that she wouldn't be going again, and handed her church-going friend a list which read:

> You are asking me to change the way I speak, the sort of music I enjoy, the length of time I usually listen to a speaker, the type of people I mix with, my body temperature, the type of chair I sit on, the type of clothes I'm used to seeing people wear, my sense of humour. You expect me to know when to stand, sit and kneel. I am prepared to change, but there was nowhere I could connect any part of my life with that service.

Ouch! But speak of change and the atmosphere can get distinctly chilly. A verger once observed to a visiting bishop: 'It's only inertia that keeps this place going!'

Sunday worship is still the shop window of the Church. It has the power to convert or to repel. For all that churchgoers say worship is an encounter with God and requires engagement from everyone present, and that it's not just Christian entertainment, the Church still has to make sure that its worship is designed and offered to the highest standard it can possibly manage. What is being offered has to be the genuine article.

'The building is cold and forbidding'

It's hard to do much about this problem, at least in the short term. Churches are hugely expensive to run and even more expensive to adapt. Sometimes it seems as if the interior design is by Stalin, heating by the

Arctic Refrigeration Co., lighting by Gloom and Sons, and soft furnishings by the prison service. Enter a church and you've stepped back 50 years in terms of contemporary design. Do you remember when high-street banks were built to look strong and secure, with marble pillars and large, impressive halls? Now we have friendly, intimate, carpeted 'shops', with customer service personnel and coffee. But churches have been more complex to adapt. Part of their glory is their 'otherness'. The Church of England alone has 16,000 churches, 13,000 of which are listed and among the most significant buildings historically and architecturally in the country. They may need toilets, kitchen facilities, new heating, lighting, and sound amplification systems. Pews require the congregation to sit in serried ranks, like old-fashioned classrooms, unable to see more than the back of someone's head. They assume a uni-directional mode of communication, and that God is located somewhere beyond the east wall. The back of the church may look like the remains of a jumble sale, with sad piles of leaflets advertising last month's events, and stacks of battered books announcing that God is prayed to in language of the seventeenth century and sung to in language of the nineteenth. The cumulative message of this kind of church can be fairly formidable – 'Don't interfere; you're here under sufferance; make the best of it.' Oh, and here's the collection plate.

'They're not my kind of people'

Now, this is a difficult one. If you're a football fan, used to spending Saturdays in exaggerated yelling after a proper liquid build-up, then feeling you'd be in a minority on a Sunday morning in church is perfectly understandable. You would be. It's possible to parody the congregation in the way one feature writer did, noting that

> . . . the churchgoers all look like the nicer characters in Australian soaps, a permanent half-smile, slightly out-of-date inexpensive clothes. The guy next to me – he's not making much of a fashion statement. He's wearing a brownish jacket, grey trousers, has shortish hair . . . the

women are wearing floral dresses to mid-calf. I would bet there are no vegetarians in the house, or people who read philosophy, or tell really good jokes in bars. These churchgoers are people I never get to meet.[2]

What the casual visitor wouldn't immediately notice is that there may well be a professor of philosophy there, there will certainly be some vegetarians, and there are probably one or two saints in the congregation whose lives would make them gasp if they but knew. But – point taken; there is a tendency in the average congregation to grey hair, safe fashion, and (occasionally) some wonderful eccentricity.

'I don't understand what's going on'

I sometimes try to imagine what it would be like if I went to a pub where, on some hidden cue, a group of men, dressed in unusual and exotic gear, got up and walked solemnly round a table three times, then sat down, sang a curious snatch of music, and lapsed into silence. This would be followed by readings from some worthy but incomprehensible ancient text, and the strained singing of a communal dirge. If this kind of behaviour continued for an hour or so I might be rather glad to escape at the end and return to the normal world where I knew roughly what was going on. In a somewhat overstated way, this may be what it seems like to someone entering a church service for the first time. Even someone returning to church after some years' absence might well lament that they didn't know where they were in the service and felt they were in a strange, new land. The net result is that newcomers can feel embarrassed and out of place when they come to church. They don't know the rules, but the message is quite clear – this place isn't for them.

So let's not underestimate the problem of going to church for very many people in our society today. Some commentators point out that this is even more tragic since people are more aware of their spiritual needs now than for many years. Writing in *The Times*, Jane Shilling commented:

It's strange that the C of E should find itself so beleaguered and diminished at a time when people, particularly the 18–30 group to whom it so desperately wants to 'reach out', are so articulate in expressing their feelings of spiritual need. The longing for spirituality is not just there in encrypted form – the feature pages' obsession with perfect bodies, perfect homes, perfect children and fuzzy mysticism – feng shui, yoga, fasting and the whole Ab Fab range of partially understood alternative spiritual disciplines. It is overt: our state of the art sound systems resonate to the sounds of chanting monks and nuns; we go on retreat to monasteries; we buy mousemats decorated with images of baby angels . . . spirituality, in short, is not a product like laceless trainers or isotonic sports drinks that we never knew we wanted. We want it, right enough. All the Church has to do is deliver. But it can't . . .[3]

Somehow the Church isn't making the connection. We assume that, deep down, people will want to come to church if we just make the odd adjustment here and there. The malaise is deeper. We've traded too long on goodwill; we've been rearranging the ecclesiastical furniture when people have been wanting God; we've often missed the cultural boat, watching it depart from our shores while we keep standing on the dockside in the illusory safety of the past.

However, one of the convictions behind this book is that the Church is beginning to engage with the more profound questions of connectedness, and is grappling positively with issues of community, spirituality, cultural relevance, freedom to grow as human beings, and so on. In fact I believe that in many, many places the local church is in remarkably good shape. It just doesn't know it.

Moreover, hundreds of millions of people all over the world do go to church regularly and positively, week by week. They don't seem to suffer any ill effects. Indeed they often seem wonderfully liberated and energized by the experience. The question might just crop up in the minds of the curious – 'Is there something we're missing?'

2

Why is going to church worth it?

⟫•◦•⟪

OK, so there are problems. Going to church is a risky business, fraught with tripwires and potential embarrassments. Nevertheless, it's one of the most common human activities in the world. In country after country churchgoing seems irresistible. There are 2,000 million people who identify with Jesus Christ and his way of life, and most of them go to church with some regularity. Why?

Because we're on a journey

It's like this: we're getting along fine, thank you very much. Education – tick. Job – tick. Life partner – tick. Housing – tick. Then something happens. It may be that it's the arrival of a child, or the death of a parent, or an encounter with illness, or the loss of a job, but something interrupts the smooth flow of personal progress. A crack appears in the concrete that has settled over our deeper lives, our questions about life, meaning and purpose. And through this crack a flower comes from nowhere. It needs to be investigated. Where shall we go to ask the right questions? Perhaps to church. Many people see their lives as a journey. Indeed, the journey motif lies deep in the human psyche. Most people have a sense of moving on and encountering new stages with new questions and tasks. Jung said that the chief task of the second half of life is to find a spiritual meaning and interpretation of the life we're living. As we turn round the corner on this journey, there, almost inevitably, will be a church.

Because we're looking for a framework to live in

There are huge gains to be found in the freedom and honesty that characterize the early twenty-first century. The internet has set off an explosion of knowledge. New technologies bring the world to our living-rooms and give us hope for all kinds of medical breakthroughs and other benefits. There is less hypocrisy, more openness and greater sensitivity to minorities. On the other hand, the exponential changes in every aspect of contemporary living have brought bewilderment and confusion to many of us as this 'future shock' reverberates through our lives. Living on the edge, as we do, brings with it the anxiety that we could tip over into primal chaos through climate change, biological and nuclear terrorism, nanotechnology that goes off the rails. We face ethical questions daily of which earlier generations simply couldn't have conceived. In many ways we've outgrown our moral and spiritual strength. Many people, therefore, turn to the Church to find a framework of values, and habits of thought and action, that offer some sanity in this spinning world. They aren't trying to escape; rather they're asking whether the ancient disciplines of the heart might not be mined afresh for a deeper wisdom to save us from individual and corporate shipwreck. It's happened before – every few centuries people discover the Church's faith afresh and wonder why nobody has ever told them about it.

Because it's a place of moral seriousness in a trivialized culture

Following on the above line of thought, many people grow weary of the absurd excesses of a culture that reduces everything – even serious discussion – to the level of entertainment. We are almost literally 'entertaining ourselves to death'. Ours is a culture where (judging by the money and media coverage involved) celebrity is more important than serious moral debate. Climate scientists tell us we're still drinking cocktails on the *Titanic* as the lifeboats are being launched. The news-stands are crowded with magazines giving us more details about the lives of B-list celebrities than we could possibly assimilate; meanwhile the ship sinks. In this context, the

Church can be a serious debater, offering thoughtful, measured and positive reflections on social and political issues. Not that everybody appreciates such contributions. Secularists want religion firmly excluded from the public arena, but most thinking people realize that the great faith traditions draw on ancient wisdom which cannot be ignored, and that religion and politics are inextricably mixed as they pursue the common good. Church, then, seems a good place to go to in order to be part of an important moral discourse. And anything is better than *Big Brother*!

Because churches make an honest attempt at community in a culture that's forgotten how to do it

As society fragments into ever tighter interest groups, church is one place where there's a genuine attempt to build a diverse, welcoming, all-age community which crosses the falsifying barriers of our common humanity and celebrates the fascinating variety of our human heritage. The fact that I have to see Edna Bucket as my sister in Christ or that I sit in my pew alongside Walter Woebegone whose theological views I regard as off the wall, means that I'm having to embody something that's essential to the well-being of society, and even the future of humanity. We have to learn to live together constructively on this crowded planet. In church we meet people of all intellectual and social backgrounds; we meet people who we would never otherwise encounter, let alone share a meal with. We meet the high achiever, the struggler, the notorious sinner and the occasional saint, the activist and the contemplative, the youthful idealist and the wizened warrior of forgotten battles. These are God's people, who you can either see as God's wounded disciples or the unlikely shock-troops of the kingdom, Both are true. They are no better and no worse than the rest of society – but they are committed to each other, in community.

Bel Mooney, writing in the *Sunday Times* at Easter, asked:

Does the Church matter? It does. 'This is our story, this is our song,' said the Revd Caroline Neill in the pulpit at the beginning of Holy Week. Looking around at babies in arms, oblivious toddlers scampering up the aisle, teenagers in jeans, the middle-aged, the elderly; contemplating the idea of sacrifice, hearing prayers for mercy and the injunction 'Go in peace', I realised two important things. First, I could not quarrel with anything in the message of the service. Second, that the feeling of community I took home with my palm cross represents far more than my neighbourhood here in Bath.[1]

When community works, it shows.

Because I'm a learner, and church seems to be a community of learners

At its best, the church knows it's a school for the learning of an earthy holiness. There's an attractive humility about such a church because it doesn't presume to have all the answers in a neatly wrapped package with a silver bow, but to be a community of learners gathered around the life of Jesus. And these learners aren't taking copious notes and preparing for exams; they're watching and trying to imitate the Main Man. It's a process of formation, not information. It's 'learning Christ' as St Paul puts it (though he puts it in the negative, 'that is not the way you learned Christ': Ephesians 4.20). One of the earliest descriptions of the Christian faith was simply 'the Way', and those who go to church and call themselves Christians certainly fall off the Way regularly. The difference is, instead of lying in the ditch and cursing the slippery path, they climb back on to it again and keep going. Make no mistake – Christians don't claim moral superiority; Jesus said, 'I have come to call not the righteous but sinners, to repentance' (Mark 2.17). And repentance is a lifelong process. We'll be learners to the end.

Because the building talks a different language, and it's fascinating

This is the opposite of one of the reasons for *not* going to church in the previous section. Here the church is a positive magnet, drawing people into its deep rhythms and its silent music. What communicates here is hard to put into words. It's just the place, the history, the prayers and dreams that have gone into it, the hopes and fears of all the years – and sometimes the sheer *space*. In our crowded lives, space is hard to find. Space to think or stop thinking, space to reflect, space to rest, to be still, to be . . . churches are past masters at this. They offer non-judgemental space for us to sift our experiences and sort out our dilemmas. They cleanse us. On a good day, with a following wind, they may even leave us feeling embraced, understood, loved. Churches can do all this without a word of worship being spoken. Hidden in this paragraph, of course, is a mute plea that churches be left open, every day, so that folk can creep in quietly and touch the edge of eternity.

Because I might strike lucky

I may get a really interesting sermon from a thoughtful priest who obviously cares about ideas, listens to what's going on in the world, and tries to make some sense of it all; and who obviously cares about God. There aren't many contexts today where you can hear a careful, well-informed and imaginative conversation between the wisdom of God in the Bible and the experience of human beings in the world. If we have preachers who are 'willing to risk body, blood, wealth and honour to preach' (Martin Luther) and who really care about how people can flourish in today's world (and who also know a thing or two about communication), then we can have in the sermon a truly enlivening, even life-changing, experience. And if it's not always like that, there's always next week!

Because I want to get in touch with God

Got there at last! I didn't want to assume too much, but this is the heart of it. The writer Julian Barnes started a Lent talk on Radio 4 in 2008 by saying: 'I don't believe in God, but I miss him.' Many people are in that position today, but some of them want to go a step further and see if they can actually get in touch with the elusive Stranger. They might even have some instinct that the psychiatrist in Peter Shaffer's play *Equus* was right when he said: 'If you don't worship you'll shrink; it's as brutal as that.' Reluctantly, perhaps, they might come to church because God might be there.

For others, worship is as natural as breathing. Mike Riddell writes:

For those whose hearts have been shafted with love, worship is as natural and as unavoidable as a tree coming into blossom with the warmth of spring. It is love language . . . The truth about us humans is that we have been made from love, and it is only in love that we discover what we are. Like a caged bird returned to the air, worship releases us into our natural environment, and we discover that we can swoop and soar and dive.[2]

Worship isn't for sycophants who seek to buy off a narcissistic God with constant affirmation; it's for people who seek to live the truth of their nature as made by God, in God, and for God – who is Love. Since 80 per cent of the world's population practise a faith, it seems that most people know this. Nevertheless, there are exceptions, and most of them live near us in the secularized West.

Because when times are hard, there are resources to be found there

You don't have to be strong all the time. The myth of constant success is a hard myth to live by but we often spend our lives trying to ascend the ladders that society puts before us. Sometimes we just run out of puff and need to sit down at the bottom of the ladder and recuperate and reassess. Strangely that's often when we encounter Christ who came down the ladder in the incarnation, and who now sits with those who can't climb any more. Churches can be places of rest, companionship and restoration. And if forgiveness needs to be part of the deal, the Church specializes in that too.

Because there's a saint or two to be found in there, and saints are exciting

Most of us are just a shadow of our future selves, and it's good to get a glimpse of what a human being is meant to be.

3

So you're going (back) to church

———⊳•⊲———

So you're going to give it a go. It's a brave decision. There's a hint of counter-cultural courage about it. You fear that people have started going to church and never been seen again – not in ordinary life anyway. They've been lost in an ecclesiastical subculture, giving up *EastEnders* for the church council meeting. There may be something dangerously addictive here. You need to know more. So what are you likely to find?

The village church

In many respects a service here is little changed from when you last went – if you did. There's the same evocative, musty smell, and the same two ladies bustling about getting everything ready, while the organist is sorting out the music and trying out a few of the tunes. However, on your way in, you noticed in the porch a picture of a four-person 'Ministry Team', whatever that is, and one smiling face with the caption 'Your local priest' and an address in the neighbouring village. You're given a hymn book and a booklet and left to sit anywhere. It's not going to be difficult to find a seat. The service proceeds with rustic informality. More people seem to be involved in leading the worship these days – it isn't a one-person monologue. And there's been some innovation too – there's a quieter water heater for the coffee, although it's still been heating up and cutting out ever since the Peace. The weekly news-sheet shows there are lots of activities going on across this cluster of parishes: training for worship leaders, a Christian learning course on 'Tough Questions', and a meeting on climate change to be held in the biggest of the six villages.

They hadn't been to church for a while, and they noticed the difference.

And there seems to be a new children's weeknight club called 'The Riot Act' (it doesn't augur well, you think . . .). Nevertheless, things have moved on. It may even be for the better.

The town centre church

Here too a lot seems reasonably familiar. There are three morning services. A quiet, said Communion at 8 a.m., using the old form of service. At 9.30 there's something called Family Worship, and at 11.15 there's Holy Communion with a robed choir. It seems that consumer choice has reached church worship too. There's a busy, purposeful feel to the church on Sunday morning – a smart news bulletin, new hymn books and a projection screen displaying 'Welcome to St Andrew's'. A music group is tuning up and then starts playing some soft gospel songs as more and more people fill up the seats (no pews now). There's also a feeling of doors having been opened to the wider community – there are prayers for the appointment of a new head teacher at the local school, and prayers too for newcomers on the estate being built on the edge of the town. The notices speak of home groups, a teddy bears' picnic, and a Leadership Team, and there also seems to be what's called a 'church plant' happening at the school (the mind boggles). There's clearly a lot going on. You notice especially an appeal for soft furnishings for a new prayer room which they hope will be open all day with resources and artefacts, music, icons, books, candles (dangerous) and lots of ideas for how to pray. Clearly spirituality is at the heart of what they do here. May be worth a return visit.

The suburban church

It has to be admitted that the building doesn't quicken the pulse. The worthy 1960s architecture leaves the church plain but open and with a strange, squeaky floor surface. The gallant congregation look to have grown gracefully old together. But their welcome is warm. Someone is setting up a Traidcraft stall to sell fairly traded goods, and someone else a stall selling recycled Christmas cards in aid of the hospice. At five to ten the priest flies in and attaches herself to the five-strong choir. They clearly try to involve both young (nine-year-old in Day-Glo trainers) and old (three servers, somewhat under-employed). The sermon hits the spot by holding together the week's news and the day's Scripture readings. People really seem to know and enjoy each other and yet they're eager to welcome a newcomer. Full marks for effort this time. You leave with a small spring in your step, although you're not sure if you've met with God or just the people of God.

The 'high' church

It looks quite forbidding at first. You pass the traumatic crucifix outside and enter a large Victorian building with a hushed atmosphere and a faint sweet smell in the air. There's also an air of quiet expectancy as you wait in the pew for something to happen, watching the white-robed servers preparing the sanctuary, always bowing as they pass the altar. There are statues of a wan-looking Mary, mother of Jesus. Then a bell is rung, the organ strikes up and the procession winds its way through the church led by a man and a boy swinging a pot on a chain (a thurible, you find out later) which belches out incense. The service is formal, highly ordered theatre. It obviously matters to people, and they know what to do, so although it's all a bit of a mystery for a newcomer, it's somehow a good mystery. There's a sense of 'otherness', something completely different and yet profoundly important. When it's over, the congregation seem to relax visibly and laughter fills the back of the church where good coffee and chocolate biscuits are served. Conversation is surprisingly normal, considering the highly esoteric experience you've just shared, and there's genuine warmth. As you leave, you think to yourself that this may not be life as we know it, but there's definitely something going on here.

The cathedral

The service ought to have a kite mark: 'Quality assured'. It's part sacred concert, part sacred theatre, in which the building has a major non-speaking part. This is seriously good worship, with everything from the sermon to the silverware on the altar being of the highest standard. There's a comfortable feeling of being able to play hide-and-seek with God in a place like this. No one is going to accost you; there certainly won't be any spiritual SATs assessment. You could come here for sheer aesthetic pleasure – but you might find yourself starting to believe. Nothing too extreme, of course; they don't do enthusiasm here, nor will there be much likelihood of revival breaking out. But minds will be stimulated, artistic senses will be nourished, and people might well inch closer to a personal relationship with God (not that they'd call it that of course). Five for artistic impression; five for content; one for welcome.

The church plant

Now what was that strange-sounding image? A 'church plant' – which has nothing to do with eccentric horticulture but everything to do with growing a new church. It meets in a school hall where the 'church' has clearly had to be set up afresh this and every Sunday morning. It feels odd and yet reassuring to come into a familiar place and see unfamiliar objects – a cross, a scattering of tea-light candles, banners, music band, PA system etc. The atmosphere is totally relaxed; the worship leader (is he ordained?) isn't wearing any robes, there's no procession, no choir, no stained-glass window. (Oh, come on! What do you expect?) But what the service lacks in recognizable rituals it makes up for in sheer enthusiasm, genuineness and noise. Children run around the wooden floor before being swept off to their Junior Church activities in nearby rooms. Suddenly you're left in a quieter space with a preacher who speaks straight from heart to heart – though if your heart is somewhere else at the time you can feel pretty detached from it all. As you drink coffee and are run into by an enthusiastic three-year-old, you reflect that this isn't a place that specializes in the numinous, but it certainly does specialize in Jesus.

The 'fresh expression'

They call it 'alternative worship' and it's certainly no Matins. The lights are atmospherically low; there's a drink to take to a comfortable low chair; soft music plays. The worship is about to explore the theme of forgiveness. There's a striking mix of film clips, poetry, mood music, structured chat, projected images, participative prayer with various optional activities, a 'cool down' period. It's full of imagination, although a bit threatening for those of a nervous disposition. Not a huge number there, but seems like a high level of personal investment from quite a few, and the age profile is encouragingly 30s. Friendly, non-precious chat afterwards. A number of midweek opportunities for practical social action, workshops, concerts etc. are projected on to the big screens. Seems like a thoughtful, accessible community. Next week perhaps?

And all of these are 'church'.

☆ ────────────────────────────────────── ☆

Follow-up for groups or individuals

Recall any visit you have made to a church in recent months. What struck you about it? How did you feel there?

If you have been going to church for a while, how would a visitor, just beginning to explore faith, experience your church? Is there anything that would strike him or her as good, very good, odd, or truly bizarre?

If you are a churchgoer, does your church offer a wide enough worship experience? If not, what would help, and is that really possible?

What would happen in your ideal church service?

☆ ────────────────────────────────────── ☆

4

Star ratings

Have you ever thought about giving star ratings to a church service? I hope, in fact, that you don't, but nevertheless if the thought did occur to you in a quiet moment when you're back in your pew after receiving Communion, I wonder if the following would be the kind of ratings you might give.

One star

The service started on time, but that's about all you could say about it. At times it seemed to be having a nervous breakdown – like when the vicar's wife had to rush home to get some bread for Communion and their dog followed her back right into the sanctuary. The service followed the book word for word; never a stray phrase risked a guest appearance. The hymns should have been strangled at birth. The sermon started with an idea but lost it early on and never found it again. The coffee was tepid. The dog ate the biscuits.

Two stars

This was a simple, ordered service. Everyone did their best but it seemed that maybe the Lord and his holy angels were playing away that day, and there was little sense of expecting God to turn up. Was this the Church of England living up to its reputation as 'the bland leading the bland'?

Mr Steel made it quite clear he did not want to share the peace.

Three stars

Some good touches here. The intercessions were very imaginative and actually gave the congregation time to pray. There was an Iona hymn which used creative imagery, and some memorable phrases in the sermon by the Reader. The service may not have been conceived as a whole, but there were some luminous moments. Pity about the choir anthem.

Four stars

The sense of anticipation was not disappointed. Lots of thought had gone into finding a balance between the formal and the informal, the known and the novel, and between different styles of music. There was dignity and simplicity about it all. The sermon had been well constructed and was well delivered, with time afterwards to reflect while some quiet flute music was played. There was a sense that what was going on was important.

Five stars

God makes a personal appearance – or nearly. The service is genuinely uplifting. There's an imaginative liturgy, wonderful music, a short, powerful sermon. There's good use of lighting and movement at different phases of the service, and thought-provoking prayers in which everyone is given a nail as we pray about the passion of Christ and the passion of the world. We go home imperceptibly but definitely changed.

The problem with star ratings of course is that they're based on the presupposition that worship is some kind of religious entertainment. And that's a death-dealing approach to worship. Worship is essentially participative. It's what happens when God reaches towards us and we reach towards God. When the meeting takes place there's a burst of divine electricity and we're energized for service. Worship is when we are caught up in the life of God. It's God's business as well as ours.

The problem is that when we look at worship from the outside, as entertainment, it's like looking through stained-glass windows from the outside of the building. The windows are black and don't allow any 'vision' of what's going on inside; you simply can't see. Similarly, when we look at worship as so-called 'objective' observers (though objectivity of this kind is actually an impossibility) we won't be able to 'see' anything – at least, nothing of the pulse and inner dynamic of worship. We have to stand *inside* the church to see the glorious colours of the stained glass, and we have to stand *inside* the experience of worship to glimpse the power and the glory of what's going on.

To change the image, it's like coming home from work and finding the living-room empty but in complete chaos, with toys strewn everywhere, cushions on the floor, a DVD playing loudly. It only makes sense when you go into the kitchen and find the children with a crowd of friends having their tea. The living-room belonged to their play; put them into it and it makes complete sense as their space. Just so, church worship makes complete sense when you put Jesus into the heart of it. Without him it might well appear chaotic and bewildering; with him it's a joyful arena of divine play.

Worship is essentially participative. You have to get inside the action, and if you do, even if it's only a 'two-star' service, you can be run down by the Hound of Heaven. God can meet you, touch you, or stop you in your tracks simply by a phrase in a Bible reading, a sentence in the prayers, the words of a hymn, the smile of a friend, the way light plays on the stone pillars, the serious concentration of a child at the altar rail, a thought that surfaces in your brain, the taste of bread and wine.

Only, you have to enter the worship.

Only enter.

☆ ───────────────────────────────────── ☆

Follow-up for groups or individuals

What services can you remember that made a real impact on you? Why was that?

What have you found most irritating about the services you have been to?

Should all services aim to have the 'Wow!' factor, or is that only for special occasions?

What can you do to ensure that you experience worship 'from the inside'?

☆ ───────────────────────────────────── ☆

5

Vicars – all shapes and sizes

———⇒•⇐———

Clergy don't come in a one-size-fits-all standard format. They come in all shapes, sizes and eccentricities. This chapter is a tribute to some of the noblest, hardest-working, most caring, thoughtful and misunderstood men and women in contemporary society.

They also have the highest ideals. They are called by a vision which is sometimes so breathtaking it is almost embarrassing to articulate. They experience human life in the raw, often stepping into places of pain and darkness that few would dare to enter. They're sacrificial and altruistic in a way that's rare these days. They work all hours and turn out on the darkest nights without a thought of renegotiating their contract (which they don't have anyway). They're physicians of the heart and poets of the soul, although they often have to be technicians of the church as well. They think about the biggest issues (God, the universe and everything) while also having to keep an eye on the parish magazine accounts and the squeak on the vestry door. They pray and ponder and love and teach and train and organize and lead worship and trouble-shoot and encourage the fallen and visit the sick and fall asleep in front of the television. And the pay is lousy.

But they are sadly misunderstood. An article in the *Sunday Times* about the 12 things you only see at Christmas led off with pantomimes, hampers, Slade, Auntie Vi, Bailey's Irish Cream and then came to 'Vicars'. It said this:

While the other main function of a church – marriage – is often taken care of in a civil ceremony these days, Christmas is inextricably linked with religion. There's no getting away from it: you can't celebrate the birth of Christ in a register office. Time, then, to meet your vicar. Once the hub of the community, vicars are for many people now some sort of eccentric curio, like a man who puts on a pith helmet and goes into the basement to 'explore Africa'. Be nice to your vicar, and remember: he probably finds you more frightening than you find him.[1]

You have to wonder how many clergy that young writer had met in the last ten years, but that's just one example of the way clergy are sometimes seen in an un-churched age. Mind you, they've always been different. In every Post Office in the Second World War a notice went up saying: 'All men between 18 and 35 are called up, except lunatics, the blind and ministers of religion'.

Sometimes, of course, the Church has set itself apart without anyone needed to help. Nepotism was not the least of the sins of the Church, but things had come to a pretty pass when Cardinal Wolsey made his school-boy son, Thomas, Dean of Wells, Provost of Beverley, Archdeacon of York, Chancellor of Salisbury, Prebendary of Wells, York, Salisbury, Lincoln and Southwell, and Rector of Rudley in Yorkshire and St Matthew's in Ipswich. Presumably he fitted his homework in between.

Change

Now, however, things have become hugely more pressurized for clergy. In the deanery of Stanhope in Weardale in 1905 there were 17 parish churches and over 30 clergy; in 2008 there were still 17 Anglican churches but now only four clergy. Since the Second World War the number of full-time parochial clergy in the Church of England has halved to around 9,000, while the population has obviously increased by millions. (There are, though, thousands more Readers, lay ministers, youth workers and so on.)

In the middle of massive social changes, one study into clergy stress found that key problematic themes kept emerging: irrelevance, isolation, guilt, low self-esteem. There are no easy answers to these long-term issues, not even the dramatic strategy displayed on balloons which were once sold

Jerry was delighted that his church was growing.

on the streets of Nigeria when the Archbishop of Canterbury was visiting. It said: 'Help the Anglican Communion. Blow up the Archbishop of Canterbury'. No. Patient work is needed to maintain the clergy in their high calling, although it's good to know that in a recent survey of job satisfaction the clergy came out second (to medical secretaries, for some reason).

There are some eternal problems associated with this public role. If a vicar visits a lot, he's too keen, but if he doesn't he's remote. If he preaches for longer than ten minutes it's too long, but if he preaches for less than ten, he can't have prepared his sermon properly. If he tells a joke in the service he's flippant, but if he doesn't, he's far too serious. If he wants the church decorated, he's extravagant, but if he doesn't, it looks shabby. If he's young, he's inexperienced, but if he's old, he ought to retire. However, when he moves on, there's never been anyone like him. Except it's as well to remember the salutary story of a vicar who told an elderly parishioner that he would be leaving the parish soon. 'But', he assured her, 'you'll probably get a better priest to follow me.' 'Not necessarily,' she replied. 'That's what the last one said before he went.'

Of course, the most memorable vicar for most people is their local priest who, for better or worse, represents the Church, and maybe even represents God. The credibility of the Christian faith usually rests in the hands of the vicar and how he or she comes across to local people at church, school, weddings, funerals, in the local press and so on. The fun is in the variety. Every priest is an ordinary person with a rich mix of gifts and fallibilities. If you cut them, do they not bleed? They are the rich mix of saints and would-be saints that you find in any group of Christians. They contain in their number both heroes and (just a few) villains – and everyone in between. What makes them distinctive, however, and very special, is that they have chosen a narrow and difficult way. By and large they don't complain about it; they just get on with loving people and trying to introduce them to the kingdom.

They are men and women of high hopes and high ideals. But they aren't God. Have mercy on them.

———————

☆ *Lord Soper was a distinguished Methodist minister who took his message to Tower Hill and then Speakers' Corner Sunday after Sunday until the very last years of his long life. On one occasion he was repeatedly heckled by someone who kept shouting out, 'What about flying saucers?' Eventually Lord Soper decided to respond. 'I'm sorry,' he said, 'but I can't deal with your domestic disputes right now.'*

☆ *The vicar was old, very devout, but sometimes far away in the service. One Sunday during Evensong, as they reached the Creed, there was silence. The curate went across to him, touched his arm gently and whispered: 'I believe in God, sir.' The vicar woke with a start. 'So do I,' he said happily. 'So do I.'*

6

Ten things to do in a boring sermon

—————➤•◄—————

The preacher has laboured long and hard to deliver his sermon. You, frankly, have done little to prepare to listen to it, but you're ready and willing. He stands up; you sit down. The prayer is said; the scene is set. There's a faint hum of expectation in the air.

But how long will your concentration last? Experience tells us that not every sermon scintillates. Revival doesn't break out every time. Some sermons are – let's face it – boring. So what then? Here's a random selection of ideas. Don't use more than one in the same sermon, unless completely desperate.

1 Practise sleeping with your eyes open. It's not easy but it's a useful transferable skill (home, office, church council, etc.).
2 Dedicate several minutes to reaching for a packet of sweets in your pocket, taking the wrapper off and getting it to your mouth, without making a noise and without anyone noticing. If you succeed, you'll feel enormous satisfaction.
3 Work out some congregational chants to liven up the service. Like this one for Anglican churches: 'What do we want?' 'Gradual change!' 'When do we want it?' 'In due course!' It's unwise to actually use the chants at this precise moment, but the fantasy will be eminently enjoyable.
4 Set yourself little problems, like: if an Anglican sermon lasts an average of 12 minutes, a Methodist sermon 16 minutes, a Roman Catholic 8 minutes and a Baptist 23 minutes; and if there are 16,000 Anglican churches each with 1.5 sermons on an average Sunday, how

many Methodist, Roman Catholic and Baptist sermons would you need to equal the total number of Anglican sermon-minutes per Sunday? And does it matter?

5 If you were bold enough, what would you say to the preacher right now, apart from 'For God's sake, stop'? And would you say it in a loud voice, or quietly with menace, or pleadingly?

6 Play the game of 'Sermon Cricket'. All you need is the weekly news-sheet and a ball-point pen. The rules are simple. Score one run every time the preacher uses the words 'church', 'money' or 'flower rota'. Score two runs for 'God' or 'Jesus' (these will be rare in some churches – don't go back next week). Score four for 'mission' or 'Rowan Williams', and six for 'R. S. Thomas'. The batsman is out if the preacher says 'eschatological', 'fresh expressions', or 'but then again, how should I know?'

7 Think of what you'll say to the preacher at the door on the way out. Favourites might be: 'Do we get time off for good behaviour next week?', 'It's a shame they make you preach so often', and 'Interesting sermon, vicar – just remind me of the point you were making' – although that is a bit of a put-down. Never apologize for snoring; the preacher may not have noticed.

8 Work out the right tone of voice for the following comment to the preacher as you leave. It's a variation on a line from Woody Allen: 'I came to listen to the sermon because I didn't understand the topic you were preaching on. I still don't understand it – but on a higher level.'

9 Set to work on adapting the titles of well-known hymns for next week's service, e.g. 'O, for a Couple of Tongues to Sing'; 'What an Acquaintance We Have in Jesus'; 'Above Average is thy Faithfulness'; 'Spirit of the Living God, Fall Somewhere Near Me'; 'Pillow of Ages, Fluffed for Me'. And maybe a choir anthem: 'I'm Fairly Certain that My Redeemer Liveth'.

10 Contemplate the Second Coming when all preaching will be un-necessary.

All this, however, is to fall in with the unfortunate but popular stereotype of the sermon as a time of patient endurance. God can use any sermon to communicate his love. Let's remember that, at its best, preaching is a powerful declaration of the acts of God, such that our minds are informed, our hearts are touched and our actions are inspired – head, heart and hands. Pray for the preacher who carries such an awesome responsibility. And pray for yourself that you can catch God's particular word for you, among the many other words that aren't.

How to get the most from a sermon

You might like to bear in mind the following points:

- The sermon is a two-way activity. Listen actively for the idea, phrase or illustration that is for you. God can use any sermon, and the humblest of his servants, to bring you his personal message. Be open; be ready; listen.
- Listen for the heartbeat of the sermon. You may be put off by the manner of delivery, the split infinitives, and the references to a film you've never heard of, but at its heart is a word from the Lord. What is it? What's the pearl of great price?
- The word that God has for you may be a word you don't want to hear. Don't screen it out. The uncomfortable words are the ones we might most need to hear and the ones our best friends have been wanting to say to us for ages.
- Don't worry if the preacher says some bizarre things; there's no need to throw out everything he or she says because of that. Equally, there will be much he or she *doesn't* say, and that might leave you frustrated. A famous theologian said that all good sermons are heresy because they so emphasize a single truth that they ignore other parallel or complementary truths and so get things out of balance. Fine – take today's pearl; there'll be another next week.
- Pray both for the preacher and for yourself. The preacher has put

him or herself heart and soul into the sermon (hopefully) and our part is to pray that the divine lightning strikes at least once.

- It can be useful to remind yourself a few minutes after the sermon what it was actually about and what you want to take out of it. Otherwise it can just get lost in the plethora of post-service activities. A timely recap might hold on to it.

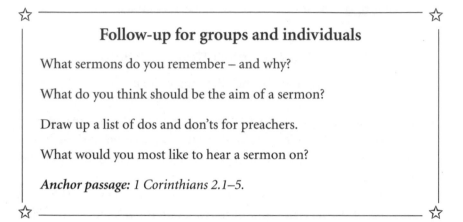

Follow-up for groups and individuals

What sermons do you remember – and why?

What do you think should be the aim of a sermon?

Draw up a list of dos and don'ts for preachers.

What would you most like to hear a sermon on?

Anchor passage: 1 Corinthians 2.1–5.

7

'The cold smell of sacred stone'

———◆———

I love musty old church buildings. That's probably partly to do with the nostalgic effect that smells have on us – pipe tobacco taking us back to a favourite grandfather, freshly cut grass reminding us of childhood holidays, a perfume that transports us to a lost romance, and so on. My family used to go to a small country village for our summer holidays and we would enter the ancient church and be greeted by the distinctive smell of old stone, crinkly prayer books and last week's flowers. It's a heady cocktail for me to this day.

To others it may be the stale smell of yesterday's faith. Philip Larkin called it 'the cold smell of sacred stone'. The piles of out-of-date leaflets and parish magazines; the unsightly bucket of crumbling oasis; the broken chair and exhausted water-heater – all of these might suggest that if God is not dead, at least he's well past his prime and spends his time at car-boot sales.

A little boy was fidgeting as the service droned on. His mother whispered: 'Hush, Martin; this is the house of God.' Martin looked around at the old pews, the stone memorials and the cobwebs. He whispered back: 'If I were God, I'd move!'

The popularity of churches

Nevertheless, for most people the actual church building is a friend they don't want to lose. A national Opinion Research Business (ORB) poll in 2003 showed that 63 per cent of the population would be very concerned if their church was no longer there; 83 per cent saw it as a place of worship and 75 per cent thought it should be used for other purposes

Humphrey had an emergency meeting with the Diocesan arsonist.

too. Most Christians would agree. Our churches ought to be given back to the community. They were built originally so that the nave could be used by the community for all sorts of events – markets and meetings, feasts and festivities. The chancel was kept for the priests to lead worship, but sacred and secular rightly occupied the same total space; they were never meant to be parted.

Stones are special to people and their communities. The broadcaster Jeremy Paxman said: 'Church spires are the great punctuation points of the English countryside. But the religious buildings of this country not only tell where we are geographically, they tell us where we've come from. They're often the only place in a community which has a living, visible connection to the past. They hot-wire us into our history.'[1] Simon Jenkins has a similar response: 'It is through the churches of England that we learn who we were and thus who we are and who we might become. Lose that learning and we lose the collective memory that is the essence of human society. We must remember.'[2]

Churches have a symbolic value far beyond their address and postcode. They carry the emotional and spiritual investment of the community, reminding us of baptisms, Midnight Mass at Christmas, prayer in time of war, weddings, funerals. These places are holy ground even for the unbeliever; they carry people's sacred memories.

Holy space

When I worked at Canterbury Cathedral I was once walking through the cloisters and saw a man sitting quietly ruminating. I greeted him gently and he came straight out and said, 'This place saved my life. Ten years ago I'd come to the end, and this place saved me.' It didn't seem right to push further. We were on holy ground.

That's why people care for these places so deeply, and commit themselves to their upkeep even if they don't go to worship. Each year 86 per cent of the population go into a church at some time: 30 per cent go to a Sunday service, 40 per cent to a baptism, 50 per cent to a wedding, and 60 per cent to a funeral. These are popular places. And when there aren't many people around, there are always the angels, crowding the rafters and brushing gently against the cheek of the person who dropped in for a quiet moment in a hectic day.

Simon Jenkins doesn't claim to be a believer, but he recognizes the power of sacred space. He writes:

The evening was warm and the gloaming was rising from the valley beneath. Through a churchyard hung low with trees I could sense the air filling with the ghosts of villagers climbing up the hill to that tiny building. I sensed their coming for a thousand years. As they arrived they hurled their hopes against those walls, wept on altars and filled the rafters with their cries. The church had received their faith, and offered in return a humble consolation. Now mute in death, these people communicated to me as they did to Eliot, 'tongued with fire beyond the language of the living'. I could not be immune to the spirits of such a place.[3]

Of course if God is as we say and present in every place, then we can meet God anywhere – on a mountain, in a living-room, in the proverbial garden. Indeed, in the United States they even have drive-in churches for you to come by car. The weekly news-sheet for one drive-in church had this wonderful request: 'Please do not start engines until the pastors have left the altar.' For most of us, however, a much-loved building acts as a porch into the presence of the divine. Space opens up; time slows down; love comes through.

There are 16,000 Anglican churches in England and Wales, of which 13,000 are listed and therefore regarded as among the most significant buildings in the country. Indeed 45 per cent of all grade-1-listed buildings are the responsibility of the churches. In that same ORB poll it appeared that 42 per cent of the population think that the State contributes significantly to their upkeep. It's true that English Heritage funds contribute very significantly to a few churches a year, but that proportion of the total annual church buildings bill is very small indeed. There is a major issue here. On the Continent the State often looks after the upkeep of church buildings, which might sound wonderful to hard-pressed parishioners faced with yet another major bill for roof repairs, but which raises other questions about losing one's soul. There's a balance to be found.

Change

The crisis comes when a church needs altering to suit the needs of a new generation and its contemporary mission. To talk about fur flying would be seriously to underestimate the ferocity now unleashed. We're now talking muskets at dawn. Pity the poor vicar who simply wants the church to be warm and welcoming to her Praise and Play toddler group. There are petitions to receive, church council meetings to defuse, anguished parishioners to calm down, and the threat of Mrs Bucket tying herself to a pew. Behind it all hangs the spectre of a sinister-sounding Consistory Court where unsuspecting vicars are boiled in oil.

Nevertheless, there has never been an era when the buildings weren't adapted to meet new needs. Aisles were built, doors and windows opened up, paintings added and removed, pews introduced (late on, usually), vestries enlarged, organs built, bells hung, fonts moved. And the Victorians, of course, practically rebuilt the whole church. Why should a new missionary impetus not mean the introduction of comfort and flexibility – heating, lighting, sound systems, chairs instead of pews, liturgical space instead of Victorian clutter? (At this point I realize that half my readers have closed this corrupt book in disgust.) But I continue: the old stones were put there for the benefit of the 'living stones' (as St Peter called the early Christians – 1 Peter 2.5), and living stones need to breathe the fresh air of the Spirit.

Most of all, of course, we now need that omnipresent facility of the modern age, the loo. And in really up-to-the-minute churches, baby-changing facilities and a crèche. In one church a text was chosen for the new facilities. It was from 1 Corinthians 15: 'We shall not all sleep but we shall all be changed.'

In truth, our church buildings have to reflect the needs of contemporary mission or they become mere museums where the spirit dies. The church is an embodiment in stone of what the living Christ says to his world. It's a theatre for life-giving worship. It's a centre for listening and forgiving. It's an arena for celebration and suffering. It's a demonstration of love in stone.

Follow-up for groups or individuals

Which churches that you have been to have spoken most powerfully to you, and why?

What strikes you most strongly about the church building you know best?

What changes would you make to the church building you know best?

What principles should guide us in balancing the integrity of a church building and the needs of the contemporary Church?

Who should be the arbiter of taste when churches are to be adapted – the church leadership, the architect, the congregation, the Diocesan Advisory Committee, the wider parish, or who?

8

Putting the Church on a larger map

Can I interest you in the rest of the family? The church family I mean. It's rather large. Of course it started rather small. There were only 11 men, sundry women, and an unknown number of people in Galilee who had met Jesus and now had plenty of undirected goodwill. Not a lot to go on. But this is what it looks like now:

- *2.1 billion:* the number of Christians in the world, 33 per cent of the world's population, comprising Roman Catholics, Protestants, Eastern Orthodox, Anglicans, Pentecostals, and many others.
- *1.1 billion:* the number of Roman Catholics, one-sixth of the world's population.
- *220–300 million:* the number of Eastern Orthodox believers, although some estimate 500 million.
- *80 million:* the number of Anglicans worldwide, in 38 provinces and with 850 bishops.
- *70,000:* the increase in the number of Christians every day worldwide (net growth).
- *600 million:* the estimated increase in the number of Christians by 2025 compared with 2000.
- *2,000:* the number of languages worldwide which have a translated portion of the Bible; 400 languages have the whole Bible.

This is in the context of 80 per cent of the world's population being adherents of one of the world's great faith traditions. About 20 per cent consider themselves atheist or agnostic. So let's see the breakdown of world religions.[1]

- Christianity: 2.1 billion, or 33 per cent of the world's population.
- Islam: 1.5 billion, or 21 per cent.
- Hinduism: 900 million, or 14 per cent.
- Buddhism: 376 million, or 5 per cent.
- Chinese traditional religion: 394 million, or 6 per cent.
- Primal indigenous religion: 300 million, or 4 per cent.
- Sikhism: 23 million, or 0.36 per cent.
- Judaism: 14 million, or 0.22 per cent. (However, a Jewish yearbook for 1991 had an entry that said 'China: population 1 billion; Jewish population: 5.' A Jewish man said to his wife: 'You can therefore be certain of two things. One, there will be six synagogues. Two, someone somewhere will say the Jews are running the country.')

Back to the Christian family. Consider this:

- The typical Christian today isn't white, middle class and from Europe or the United States. The typical Christian is young, female, black, and from the global south.
- Western Europe is the only part of the world where the Christian faith is struggling. Everywhere else the Church is growing, especially in South America, Africa, and South-East Asia. It is said there are 10,000 new Christians every day in China.
- In the United States less than 1 per cent claim to be agnostic or atheist.
- The Anglican Church in Nigeria has had to double the number of dioceses in the last ten years to cope with the growth of the Church.

What this is saying is that wherever we go in the world there are members of the family. They may meet in a suburban church in an English city, in a cool corner of an Indian village, in a purpose-built mega-church in

Korea, under a tree on the edge of the desert in southern Africa, in a mock-Gothic cathedral in North America, in a snowbound community room in Alaska, in a tin church in a shanty town in South America, in a prison chapel or a school hall or a front room anywhere.

And best of all, the same thing is happening in a church near you!

For example, in the Church of England:[2]

- *1.7 million:* the number of people who attend a Church of England service each month, with around 1 million attending each Sunday.
- *2.8 million:* the number of people who attend church on Christmas Eve or Christmas Day; 43 per cent of the population attend church some time over the Christmas period (more in London).
- *47 per cent:* the proportion of adults attending a funeral or memorial service. Those entering a church to find a quiet space totalled 21 per cent. Both figures are rising year on year.
- *86 per cent:* the proportion of the population visiting a church in the course of a year for one of many reasons.
- *12.5 million:* the number of people visiting a Church of England cathedral each year. Three of England's top five historic 'visitor attractions' are Canterbury Cathedral, York Minster and Westminster Abbey.

And while we're about it:

- *23 million:* the number of hours of voluntary service *outside* the church which are given each month by churchgoers.
- *515,000:* the number of under-16-year-olds involved in activities provided by the Church of England *outside* church worship.
- *1 million:* (just over) the number of children educated in Church of England schools.

The Church is alive, well and busy.

9

Ten things you never hear said in church

⟫•0•⟪

There are many things you hear said in church, ranging from the beautiful to the scandalous. Here are some things you never hear said – unless you're in a very strange church indeed.

1 'I love it when we sing hymns I've never heard before.'
2 'I'm so excited about the 52-week sermon course on Leviticus.'
3 'I don't think the vicar ought to try "House of the Rising Sun" at the Family Service again.'
4 'It's my turn to sit in the front pew.'
5 'I was so enjoying the sermon I completely forgot I was due on the golf course at noon.'
6 'Vicar, we'd like to send you on this month-long training course in the Bahamas.'
7 'I volunteer to be a permanent teacher in the Sunday School.'
8 'The Annual Church Meeting – it's the highlight of my year.'
9 'I always feel better after I've doubled my annual stewardship pledge.'
10 'Jesus who?'

Please feel free to add to this list in the space below:

PART 2

The Church as it should be

10

Q: What's the Church for?
A: Worship

⟶•⟵

I'm going to set the bar quite high here. The primary task of the Church is to worship. We come to church for all sorts of reasons, some of which hardly bear repeating in respectable company, but the Church itself, the Church as a whole, the Church in its pure, uncut form, is there to worship God. We may be there because we like the vicar, want the baby baptized ('christened', your mother-in-law called it), made a bargain with God while in hospital, want little Joel to go to a church school, just got the feeling we ought to, lost the toss – all sorts of reasons.

But there's no getting away from it: worship is about God, not us. Hard as it is to tear ourselves away from the narcissistic mirror, worship is meant to be the moment of truth when the One who we might have dimly remembered through the week blazes into full focus. In worship we celebrate God, the Source of life. It's the time in the week when we get it right for once, when we let God be God and de-throne our idols, chief of which is our own ego. Worship is what we exist for. I worship; therefore I am.

Now, this could come across as a somewhat worrying idea. Does this suggest that God is an immature despot who needs constant congratulations to keep himself going, a B-list celebrity who can't exist without fawning fans? Absolutely not! We need to worship in order to find out who we truly are. Worship is for *our* health, not God's. St Augustine said: 'O God, you have made us for yourself, and our souls are restless until they find their rest in you.' We are worshipping beings, but if we deflect our worship on to those things that are not God, then we change the value of everything, swap the price tickets on every item in the store, and 'worship the creature and not the Creator'. That way lies self-destruction.

Moreover, we worship not just for ourselves but for the whole world, in order to keep the world on course. We'll never have everyone coming to church on Sunday morning, not should we expect them to. We worship on their behalf, holding them and all the things they do, before God. It's a huge privilege.

All this means that the *form* of worship isn't as important as the *fact* of worship. The acid test is whether an act of worship is truly alive and life-giving, not whether it's liturgically perfect. A Christian from South America had visited England and was invited to tell a meeting back home what had impressed him about the Church in Britain. He replied: 'All the services start punctually. Even if the Spirit hasn't arrived yet!' It's the Spirit who gives life to worship. What matters is not what form of words we use but that our spirits are ignited by divine fire. Wherever the worship goes and whatever its shape, what really matters is that we catch the tail of the divine tiger, and hold on.

Where worship starts

Worship starts in human wonder and ends in holy obedience. It starts with an awakening of the sleeping beauty of our wonder at the sheer miracle of life. It's the 'is-ness' of things that sometimes stops us in our tracks. A child, freshly minted from the womb, a leaf on the turn, a friendship beyond words, a mountain scraping the sky. The poet Rilke said: 'One thing, truly experienced, even once, is enough for a lifetime.' All this wonder we can bring into worship in our own church, so that we are in the frame of mind to encounter the even greater wonder that is Jesus Christ. But how can we pour infinity into a pint pot?

As we get caught up in worship we find that it's a kind of glad shout of celebration, like the 'Yes' on our lips when our side scores a goal, or the 'Yes' in our heart when the last note of the symphony echoes around the concert hall. It's the 'Yes' we feel when we fall in love and we'd do anything for the one we love. Worship is our 'Yes' to life and to God, in the midst of many voices that tell us to keep quiet or to keep our preferences to ourselves. It's a shout of exhilaration and gratitude.

The disk with the words went missing again.

That's the theory anyway. The reality can be rather different. On a wet Sunday morning in February when there's a pile of work to be done and the sun hasn't shone since 1966, it's often hard to raise a 'Yes'. 'If you say so', or 'Whatever' feels nearer the mark. Nevertheless, making the effort to put ourselves into a place of glad gratitude is nearly always worthwhile. It changes our point of view. It says: 'This is what I was made for. This is where I'm meant to be.' And gradually, oh so gradually, we become a fraction more like the one we worship. It's always like that. As Tom Wright puts it: 'Those who worship money become, eventually, human calculating machines. Those who worship sex become obsessed with their own attractiveness or prowess. Those who worship power become more and more ruthless.'[1] But those who worship Jesus Christ become, all unaware, more and more like him, though very slowly, in small gradations. And the world needs them.

Of course there are all sorts of strange practices that we experience in worship. The dress code is one, in Anglican churches at least. As a Bishop I wear a mitre at special services. At one such service I heard a little girl say to her mother, 'Mummy, is that man a chef?' But special clothes help to make it a special occasion. We aren't just popping down to the shops; we're meeting the Lord of Hosts. Moreover, rituals develop in order to mark special situations, whether that be a wedding, a cup final, a funeral, or a graduation. We are ritual-making people. It's worth taking time to find out why church practices in worship, and elsewhere, have developed as they have.

Soul food

If worship starts in human wonder, it ends in holy obedience. But in between there's a journey, and that journey takes in, primarily, Scripture and sacrament, undergirded by prayer. Scripture is soul food, and sacrament is soul music. Let's see what that means.

We need *soul food* to eat, regularly. The Bible was written by many hands over a period of a thousand years and is a distinctly diverse and complex set of writings, comprising history and ancient tales, wise sayings and prayers, poetry and rules of the road, warnings and wild dreams, letters, and that strange new *genre* 'Gospels'. But through it all, people hear God speaking to them, and always have. This is the word made readable, which points us to the Word made flesh (Jesus).

Of course we have to navigate deep, disturbing waters on the way. Why did God have it in for the Amalekites? Is the rape of Tamar by her half-brother suitable material for public reading? When Jael hammered a tent peg through Sisera's head, was that done to the glory of God? It's all lively stuff, and indeed it's all for us to work on even when we don't understand it or are puzzled by it. Through the extraordinarily diverse narratives of scripture we taste the huge variety of dishes which together give the full and balanced diet of soul food on which the world has feasted for centuries. One theologian called the Bible 'food for wrestlers'. Equally it's food for scholars, for seekers, for lovers and for simple followers. I expect to be grappling with the profound complexity of the Bible till the end of my life.

Soul music

The sacrament of Holy Communion takes us into the world of *soul music*. I don't mean literal music; I mean that here in the sacrament are gifts that make the heart sing. Christ comes to us through bread and wine. We need symbols to encounter God because we couldn't stand the full charge of divine electricity without protection. Bread and wine are the ordinary, innocent things that Jesus chose as the means by which to give us his life. He promised this at the last supper he had with his friends. Now he calls *us* his friends as well (John 15.15), and shares his inexhaustible life with us. I can't think of a greater privilege.

And this service of Holy Communion, or the Mass, or the Eucharist or the Lord's Supper, has fascinated and empowered millions of Christians ever since that first shared meal on a dark night in Jerusalem. It was a sad song the disciples sang that night, but after the amazing events of Easter, Ascension and Pentecost, that song has gone out into all the world as the victory song of the people of God – truly 'soul music' for the Church. I've sung that music on a mountainside in Scotland with the wind flapping the tent door to reveal glory outside and glory inside. I've sung it under a solitary tree in a wide, burning basin in the Sinai desert on Low Sunday, enjoying 'Thine be the Glory' and sharing the Peace with four bemused Bedouin. I've sung it at the high altar in Canterbury Cathedral, and by my father's death-bed, in a caravan in the south of France, and by the Sea of Galilee with water lapping my feet. And never better than on a thousand Sundays in ordinary parishes in Birmingham, Somerset, Durham, Canterbury and Oxford with the faithful people of God.

And always the question I ask myself is the one posed by the former

Archbishop of Canterbury Michael Ramsey: 'The supreme question is not what we make of the Eucharist, but what the Eucharist is making of us.' How are we being made into people who make things change? How effectively are we singing the Lord's song in a strange land?

The 'end' of worship

This is where 'holy obedience' makes its appearance as the trajectory of worship. Certainly worship is about God, for God and to God. It starts with holy wonder and takes a path through Scripture and sacrament to the very heart of God's love for the world. But eventually it has to emerge in people who have been changed by the encounter. Then we're ready to set off into the thick of everyday life where people struggle to survive, to cope, to laugh, to thrive. Our task is to join in with God's great project of making a new world out of the debris of the old. We have to give him the best raw materials ('debris') we can provide. We offer all of ourselves to all God has revealed himself to be, for the sake of all we know of the world.

And it's our worship that keeps us on course.

☆ ──────────────────────────────── ☆

Follow-up for groups and individuals

Look at the chapter 'Star ratings'. Which of the examples is nearest your recent experience of worship, and why?

Has there been a time when you felt you have encountered God in worship? Where and when was that, and what happened?

What to you are the essential ingredients of good worship, and what is secondary?

Anchor passage: can you deduce any principles for worship from Revelation 5.6–14?

☆ ──────────────────────────────── ☆

11

Q: What's the Church for?
A: Mission

If the Church's first task is to worship God, its second task is to join in God's mission. The last five words are important. The mission is God's, and it's something we join in rather than construct for ourselves. God's very nature is to be missionary because mission is the outpouring of God's love into his world. We are simply (ah – 'simply'!) called to join in with what God is doing. It follows that 'the God of mission has a Church, not the Church of God has a mission'.

The problem has so often been that a church has felt it 'ought' to have 'a mission', and the results have been disappointing. We had the mission, and enthusiasm has been limited; only the keen ones have been bright-eyed and bushy-tailed. Most people kept their heads down until the danger passed. Results have been mediocre and needed a particular spin from the vicar at the Annual Church Meeting. Everyone breathed a sigh of relief when next year's project was back to refurbishing the church hall.

But if mission is actually sharing in the overflow of God's love through-out the world, then it's a much happier thought. For one thing, we're already on the winning side! Moreover, mission then becomes a way of doing everything, rather than a special activity.

Mission is:

- telling the world it's loved;
- telling a story about new life in a culture obsessed with death;
- embracing the pain of others rather than watching it on TV;
- sharing my faith journey when it seems welcome;
- one beggar telling another beggar where to find bread;

- a whisper of faith in the face of disaster;
- remembering it's people, not statistics, who feel hunger;
- a smile, a wave, a cup of tea;
- living the way of Jesus with humanity, vulnerability and non-violence;
- a God who chooses for his kingdom tax-collectors and junkies, hookers and layabouts, car thieves, Chelsea supporters, the cast of *Coronation Street*, traffic wardens and bishops. What's wrong with this God? Has he no taste?

Anglican churches around the world have been working with a particular definition of mission for a few years now, and it seems to bear the weight of experience. It identifies five *marks of mission*.

The work of the Church is the mission of Christ:

1 To proclaim the good news of the kingdom (equals – to tell people about God's love).
2 To teach, baptize and nurture new believers (equals – to help new Christians grow in faith).
3 To respond to human need by loving service (equals – to love people!).
4 To seek to transform the unjust structures of society (equals – to change the world).
5 To strive to safeguard the integrity of creation, and sustain and renew the face of the earth (equals to look after the environment).

To proclaim the good news of the kingdom

This is bottom-line evangelism. Please don't be scared. Someone got you as far as reading this book. Or someone passed on the faith to you, whenever that was. It might have been a loving parent or a good friend or a youth leader, but someone said certain things or lived a certain way, and the result is that you and I have moved some distance along a faith journey. Sometimes faith has been around us all the time. Sometimes it has come from a silent struggle to make sense of things. Sometimes it

As the vicar alarm went off, the Robinsons dived for cover.

has come from a challenging question. I was at college with a man who had been an Olympic athlete at 400 metres. One day a Christian said to him, 'Why do you spend your whole life running round in circles?' He's now ordained.

The freedom that Jesus gives to people is such good news it has to be shared. Jesus showed his contemporaries what it was like to live a life that was full to the brim. His freedom was too much for the authorities and he was killed as a major threat to civic order, but in dying he faced evil head on and drained it of its poison, for us as well as for himself. To demonstrate that victory, God raised him from the dead and showered his people with his Spirit. The kingdom of God – a new way of living with God at the centre – has now broken into the world through all that

Jesus did, and his freedom is there for the taking. Of course the 'liquid gold' of this gospel has to be poured into the new moulds of today's culture. Presentation can't stand still. But the Church can't simply file away the good news of Jesus under 'J'. If I found a cure for cancer I'd be wanting to share it as widely and freely as possible.

When you go to church there's always good news in the air.

To teach, baptize and nurture new believers

The journey to faith is often through some form of nurture group. We begin to notice deeper questions forming in our mind – some disturbance of the mental landscape – and so we join a group to find out more. Suitable courses have proliferated in recent years – Alpha, Emmaus, Start, Christianity Explored, Credo – and they offer the opportunity for teaching, questioning, thinking, moving along. And at some point there may come a point of discovery or commitment, a point where we say 'Yes, I'm OK about this, I'm in.' Bishop Stephen Cottrell helpfully says the Church acts like a midwife, accompanying our journey in which, as in childbirth, the mother herself does most of the work. But finally there comes a point where the midwife/Church has to say 'Push!' That's when we have the new birth.

Then, as followers of Jesus, we have to continue the journey towards maturity for the rest of our lives. The baby grows – or else it dies. Paul in one of his letters talks about the goal of our lives being that we attain 'the full stature of Christ' (Ephesians 4.13). The full stature of Christ seems to have evaded most of us, so growth is our continuing agenda. Resources are everywhere, but living close to Christ through prayer, reading the Bible, and generally struggling to be holy, is the start. Moreover the Church is knee-deep in books, courses, DVDs, on-line learning, retreats, pilgrimages, prayer schools and the like. These things will help, but when our life is over we'll never have done any more than dip a toe into the ocean of God's loving reality.

But going to church gets us on to the beach.

To respond to human need by loving service

The test of a Christian life, we are told by Jesus, isn't how pious we are but how we care for the hungry and thirsty, the stranger and the destitute, the prisoner and all in need (Matthew 25.31–46). Living as we do in a world deluged and saturated with words and good intentions, Christians are called to embody their words in tangible action for the good of others. Not just love, but 'love with skin on it'.

I find it humbling to see how far my fellow Christians go to follow the command of Jesus to love both their neighbour and their enemy. I see them running schools and literacy classes, orphanages and employment workshops, HIV/AIDs programmes and fair-trade initiatives. Over 40 per cent of primary health care in Africa is delivered by the churches. Christians are found in the places of deepest pain and darkness, and they stay there when the cameras have moved on. They're in the slums; they're with the homeless and the dying; they're in the refugee centres and alongside the asylum-seekers. They founded the Samaritans, Amnesty, Oxfam, the Children's Society and the hospice movement. They're all over the place, bringing light into darkness.

And best of all, Christians, with others of goodwill and good faith, do a million acts of kindness a day, right where they are. It's not for nothing that, in Nick Hornby's novel *How to be Good*, when her husband suddenly starts to act with uncharacteristic generosity and altruism, Katie tries to understand what's happened by first of all going to church. Is that the secret? It certainly should be.

Writing in *The Guardian* in 2008, Simon Jenkins said:

Whenever I have visited poor places – such as Salford, St Paul's, Bristol, or London's Poplar – and wondered to whom the desperate turn in time of need, the finger points to the Church. Of all voluntary institutions, those based on religion are the most present and the most committed. One reason is that the parish priest is the last profession that still rates it essential to live among its clients. All the rest have fled.[1]

Going to church should be a major source of energy for a life of compassion and care.

To seek to transform the unjust structures of society

In his acceptance speech for the Nobel Prize for literature in 1980, Czeslaw Milosz said: 'In a room where people unanimously maintain a conspiracy of silence, one word of truth sounds like a pistol shot.' One of the mission tasks of the Church is to sound that pistol shot when society is disordered and the structures are diseased. It cannot be right that one billion people in our world live on less than a dollar a day. It cannot be right that a child dies of malaria in sub-Saharan Africa every 30 seconds. It cannot be right that 6 per cent of the population of the world possesses nearly 60 per cent of its wealth. Why do 75 per cent of the UK's prisoners who serve less than six months reoffend? Why does the UK spend £400 million a year on drug rehabilitation and have only a 3 per cent success rate? There are deep, structural problems with the way society is ordered.

Desmond Tutu once famously said: 'I am puzzled about which Bible people are reading when they suggest religion and politics don't mix.' Clearly the Bible is packed with God's interactions with the social and political affairs of God's people. God's concern is with human flourishing and the welfare of communities, and that immediately takes the Church into issues of where power is exercised and how fairly that is done – whether in apartheid South Africa, communist Eastern Europe, or in globalized economies everywhere. And as the theologian Karl Barth wrote: 'To clasp the hands in prayer is the beginning of an uprising against the disorder of the world.'

I once got a card with the caption: 'I tried to change the world, but I couldn't find a babysitter.' Changing the world alone can be a challenge. Doing so in the company of a large group (maybe millions) of other Christians makes it seem possible. And it starts in a church near you.

To strive to safeguard the integrity of creation, and sustain and renew the life of the earth

Like many of us, the earth has a very thin skin. What's going on in that narrow strip of protective and productive air-space is hugely worrying.

Climate change is said to be happening so quickly that it's been said we're on the *Titanic*, we've hit the iceberg, and we have just five years (maybe ten) to get off. The facts of climate change are well known and don't need rehearsing here. The implications are not just in the realm of disastrous weather changes and human suffering through drought and hunger, but also in mass migration and global insecurity. And, as ever, the poor will pay the price for the rich.

Christians have a clear mandate to contribute to the answer, in part because Christian theology is much concerned with humanity's wise stewardship of creation and the goal of a world living in God's harmonious *shalom*. It's also clear that while technology and wiser consumption of the world's resources have part of the answer, the world's great faiths are perhaps the only levers powerful enough to move the rusty hinges of the human heart to make the sacrifices necessary for collective survival. In this context 'loving our neighbour' means loving our grandchildren whose world we are making nearly uninhabitable.

Human beings are not invaders of a world to be conquered and exploited, but integral parts of the web of creation, and we therefore need a theology of 'Enough'. Creation didn't fall; humanity did, and it's humanity that needs to repent of its greed, consumerism and over-indulgence. The exhausted earth simply can't afford more Europeans and Americans. Here is a cause worthy of high Christian commitment, and it starts when we read the Scriptures with fresh eyes and receive bread and wine as the first-fruits of a world ordered in harmony with itself and its loving Creator.

It has been suggested that in a world congested with issues of faith, a sixth mark of mission should be about dialogue and conversation with people of other world faiths. Certainly there is an urgency about these relationships, for the sake of the world. Christians will need to embody the grace, generosity and hospitality of God while not compromising their core beliefs. Gentleness, honesty and integrity are crucial as we share the stories that shape us at the most basic levels of belief and action.

Do these *marks of mission* attract you? Because that's what the Church is called to do. It's a superb vision, worthy of everything a human being has got. But it has to be worked out in the ordinary details of daily living.

And that's the rub.

☆ *A man is met at the gates of heaven by St Peter.*

> Peter: *I don't know if you realize that we have a points system before you*
>   *can get into heaven; you need 100 points from your life on earth.*
> Man: *Well, I lived with my wife faithfully for 50 years and never looked*
>   *at another woman. Will that help me?*
> Peter: *Very good, three points.*
> Man: *I went to church every week and tithed my income.*
> Peter: *Good, well done, two points.*
> Man: (getting frustrated) *I organized a gift of clothing to AIDS orphans*
>   *in Africa.*
> Peter: *Excellent, three points.*
> Man: *But I've only got eight points. I'll never get there but for the grace*
>   *of God.*
> Peter: *Excellent. Come in!*

Follow-up for groups and individuals

Which of the five marks of mission are you most drawn to, and which most scared of? Why?

Which mark of mission do you think your local church does best, and which least well?

If you are a regular churchgoer, take each of the marks of mission and ask 'What does this one mean for us here and now?'

Do you think relations with other world faiths are crucial enough now to become a sixth mark of mission?

What would you like to do, either individually or collectively, out of these discussions?

12

Q: What's the Church for?
A: Community

———◆———

There's a growing frustration with our fragmented, individualistic, consumer-oriented ways of living at the start of the twenty-first century. A young city trader called Geraint Anderson gave up his job and accompanying lifestyle in 2007. He'd done ten years and it had begun to sicken him. A year later this is what he said of his move.

> The revolution has to be in our hearts and souls. City boys need to pay their taxes, stop stealing off us and stop their consumption. Give some money to charity. And have one Ferrari, not three. I'd like to set up a commune in Pembrokeshire. I'd like to show people an alternative to this system where you get rich or die trying. I'm going to try and do something to improve the situation. Although it's just idealistic nonsense, I don't care. I prefer to be part of the solution than part of the problem. I will fail, but I hope there will be some kind of nobility in the failure.[1]

He may not, indeed, persuade the world by himself or in his commune, but a lot of other people share the frustration, and are looking in other directions as they try to answer the question, 'How then shall we live?' Advance warning of the problems piling up ahead came in a famous paragraph at the end of philosopher Alasdair MacIntyre's book *After Virtue*, where he said:

> What matters at this stage is the construction of local forms of community within which civility and intellectual and moral life can be

sustained through the new dark ages which are already upon us . . . this time however the barbarians are not waiting beyond the frontiers. They have already been amongst us quite some time and it is our lack of consciousness of this that constitutes part of our predicament. We are waiting not for Godot but for another doubtless very different St Benedict.[2]

Coming from very different backgrounds, both these voices are pointing us towards community as the vital form of social existence which offers hope in our divided, competitive and ruinously consumerist culture. It shouldn't be surprising that the great world faiths have known about this for centuries. The Church has known the importance of community from the early days of monastic life in the north African desert. Further shaped by Benedict, Dominic, Francis and others, religious communities have been one of the mainstays of the Church through the Christian centuries, and in many ways the praying heart of the Church.

However, it has also been the genius of the Christian faith to emphasize the importance of local congregations, not just in monastic life but wherever 'church' has sprung up. When people become Christians they very rarely do so on their own; they have been known, loved, accompanied and encouraged by a community of faithful people – the local church. Community is the Church's mode of existence. Communities are the human expression of divine love, showing us what God wants for us and valuing us for who we are. It's in a community that people know our name.

So when we start going to church we're not just engaging in a particular kind of activity, we're entering a community. This may be alarming because we don't want to get too close to the remarkable, diverse and sometimes odd assortment of people God has called to be the church in that place. If the church is spiritually and socially intelligent it will understand and respect our caution, but the hope is that we would come to value and rejoice in the sheer richness of this unlikely community, and that eventually we might give ourselves to it with something like glad abandon. The 'unlikeliness' is the delight. It's in meeting the unexpected and different that we are stretched, surprised and enriched by a God of all cultures, classes and backgrounds. Where else would you get such diversity in our 'must-fit-me', self-selecting society?

The shape of community

Brother Sam of the Franciscans wrote an article in 1998 that has echoed in my mind ever since. In it he said:

> Monastic life may seem utterly out of tune with the spirit of our times, yet if we are entering another dark age it may be to the wisdom of such a way that the Church of today needs to turn. I sense that the renewal of both Church and society will come through the re-emerging of forms of Christian community that are homes of generous hospitality, places of challenging reconciliation, and centres of attentiveness to the living God.[3]

Hospitality, social justice and holiness. That's a powerful combination, and it's the call of every local congregation. Does that attract you to the church? I hope so, because every one of us has something to contribute to that vision for the local church.

Homes of generous hospitality

Church doors ought to be physically and metaphorically flung wide open. There is no human being who is not welcome in God's family. Sadly, human beings have a fatal facility for grading people in terms of their acceptability, and even churches slip into this insidious habit. If you are single, black, gay, unemployed, have a disability, or are in some other way 'different' from the prevailing culture of the church, you may be treated in a barely observable but definitely 'other' way. It won't be intended, but it may need your patience and forgiveness. Jonathan Sacks calls our local communities 'workshops of virtue'. We're still being shaped in the workshop. We're work in progress, but the goal is clear – we need to be places known for the warmth and acceptance of our welcome, and the way we value every person bringing their own gift, for none of us is ungifted.

Places of challenging reconciliation

In a global culture that's becoming ever more divided and fractious, it's becoming clear that one of the main roles of the Church is healing and holding together. In terms of God's great project of drawing all things together in Christ, 'reconciling the world to himself' (2 Corinthians 5.19), every act of love towards the world is part of that reconciliation. The local church is therefore called to engage with its community in service, compassion, advocacy, and social and political action. I love it when I find Christians involved in visiting schemes, credit unions, lunch clubs, food banks, eco-congregations, prison visiting, work with the homeless and mentally disabled, and the like. Where the wider community suffers, we suffer; where it flourishes, we flourish. This is really back to basic beliefs, such as loving God and loving our neighbour, seeing the Church as 'the only community that exists for those who aren't its members', and believing that we'll find Jesus in the next person we meet. We know all this. We just have to try and do it.

Centres of attentiveness to the living God

Christian communities need to be committed at the centre and loose at the edges. Commitment at the centre means having our roots deeply earthed in God. This is where the distinctiveness of Christian communities should begin to show up most clearly. The local church needs to have a holy fascination for God, a deep thirst, an irrepressible joy in God's company. This shouldn't be a self-conscious absorption in things spiritual, just as the best marriages aren't cloying and introverted but profoundly welcoming and natural, but it should be obvious to anyone who chances upon these people that the most important Person here, the One around whom everything happens, isn't visible. God is the constant 'play-maker', and the source of endless energy, creativity and fun, but only visible out of the corner of one's eye, only recognized when he's just left. But if you and I, as new people in this church, don't become aware of the extra dimension to everything that happens here, then it will have to be said that the church has failed to be itself. Christ is the invisible magnet, the elusive Stranger, the divine Storyteller, the gentle Persuader, whom we all seek. If we miss Jesus, we've missed everything.

Jesus-in-community

After he had clarified his vocation through his baptism in the Jordan and his retreat in the desert, the first thing Jesus did was to gather a community around him. From then on it was always Jesus-in-community. It was a fragile community, and eventually every one of his chosen friends deserted him and needed to be re-gathered in the Upper Room after the resurrection and given the promised power of Jesus' presence in order to set off to tell the world. Nevertheless, Jesus knew his had to be both a personal and a collaborative ministry. Until the end it was always Jesus-in-community.

Notice also that what Jesus left us wasn't a set of rules or instructions, not a creed or box of doctrines. He left a community. It was a huge risk. An old legend has Jesus returning to heaven when it was all over and meeting two archangels. They said to him: 'Welcome back, Jesus. That was tough. How is the work going to carry on?' Jesus replied: 'No problem. I've left Peter and the others to carry it on.' 'You cannot be serious,' said the archangels (thus pre-dating John McEnroe by several centuries). 'That crowd of failures who all let you down?' 'Well,' said Jesus, 'I have no other plans.'

Nor does he. We are it. There's no plan B. In particular we are, in St Paul's colourful phrase, 'the Body of Christ'. So we remain Jesus-in-community, his continuing Body. It's the community's responsibility to carry on the work of Christ, preparing the ground for the once-and-future King to claim his own land as a new creation.

But we have to admit that here, in its hundreds of thousands of communities, the Church is at its strongest and weakest. The local church can seem like a battlefield strewn with bodies, or like a taste of heaven. And this of course is what people see of the Christian faith and what they judge it by. There's a tremendous responsibility on church leaders in every community to work hard at shaping healthy, attractive, compelling 'communities of grace'. These communities need to hum with the divine presence. They need occasionally to leave people saying, 'Wow! What have they got?' (Or even, 'What are they on?')

That doesn't mean they won't experience conflict. Conflict can be the sign of a lively, engaged and searching community, hammering out important issues on the road of discipleship. I would much prefer that kind of community to a quiescent one where no one has the interest or energy to debate or disagree. The crucial quality the church needs to exhibit is that it's *alive*, and alive with the life of Christ. Then people are attracted to come and see what's going on, and maybe to walk alongside, and eventually to walk *inside*, and find a home.

A healthy church

What are the signs of such a church, one that looks and feels healthy? When I was a vicar I used to take the community's temperature incessantly – too much, indeed. But I wanted to know whether it felt healthy. A healthy body can try anything; so too a healthy body of Christ. So what does one look for? Work done over a number of years by Robert Warren and others has yielded the following characteristics.[4] A healthy church:

- *Is energized by faith*, rather than just keeping things going and trying to survive. This will be reflected in the quality of worship, engagement with Scripture and the nurturing of faith journeys.
- *Has an outward-looking focus*, with a whole-of-life rather than a church-life concern. It's rooted in the community, passionate about social justice and makes connections between faith and daily living.
- *Seeks to find out what God wants*, rather than trying to please everybody. It takes seriously the tasks of building vision, prioritizing mission and discerning vocations.

- *Faces the cost of change and growth*, rather than resisting change and fearing failure. It takes risks, responds positively to problems, and affirms good experiences of change.
- *Operates as a community*, rather than functioning as a religious club. Relationships are nurtured, and lay ministry and shared leadership teams are seen as vital.
- *Makes room for all*, being inclusive in its welcome to children and young people, enquirers and people from all different backgrounds, abilities and ages.
- *Does a few things and does them well*, especially in worship, pastoral care, baptisms, weddings and funerals, and administration. It embodies good news and enjoys itself, being relaxed about what isn't being done.

It's a good checklist, and when someone is new to a church they often have a clearer view of its health than they have later when they've become habituated to its life.

Above all, it's the quality of community that counts. In the West we've got used to saying: 'I think, therefore I am.' In Africa – where they know a thing or two about community – they prefer: 'We belong, therefore I am.'

From the Epistle to Diognetus, *c.* AD 124:

Christians are indistinguishable from other people by nationality, language or customs. They do not inhabit separate cities of their own, or speak in a strange dialect, or follow some outlandish way of life. Unlike some other people, they champion no purely human doctrine. With regard to dress, food and manner of life, they follow the customs of whatever city they happen to be living in, whether it's Greek or foreign. And yet there's something extraordinary about their lives. Any country can be their homeland, but for them their homeland, wherever it may be, is a foreign country. They live in the flesh but they are not governed by the desires of the flesh. They pass their days upon earth, but they are citizens of heaven. Obedient to the laws, they yet live on a level that transcends the law ... In short, what the soul is in the body, Christians are in the world ... God has appointed them to this great calling, and it would be wrong for them to decline it.

☆ *The wise old Mother Superior was dying. The nuns gathered around her bed. She asked for a little warm milk to sip, so a nun went to the kitchen to warm some milk. There too was a bottle of whisky from last Christmas, so she poured a generous amount into the warm milk. Mother drank a little, then a little more, and then she finished it all down to the last drop. 'Mother,' the nuns said, 'give us some of your wisdom before you die.' The Mother Superior raised herself up in bed with a pious look on her face, and pointed out of the window. 'Don't sell that cow,' she said.*

Follow-up for groups or individuals

What has been your best experience of community, anywhere, not necessarily in church? Why was it so?

What are the most important characteristics of the church community you know best? List them individually and then compare them together.

Compare your list with the Healthy Churches list above. What is the significance of any variations?

What three priorities would you advocate and commit to, to help the health of the local church?

Anchor passages: Acts 2.41–47; 1 Corinthians 1.10–31; Colossians 3.12–17. What do these passages teach about Christian community, and how can they be applied and lived today?

13

Q: What's the Church for?
A: Restoring the sacred centre

———— ❦ ————

In the previous three chapters I've been asking the question: 'What's the Church for?' and I've given three answers – worship, mission and community. If you imagine those three as interlocking circles, there is an overlap between the circles in the centre. That's where I would place a fourth answer to the question: one of the Church's chief concerns is to restore the sacred centre – in ourselves and in society at large.

The need

The need is obvious. Limitless technology and endless consumption have led us to a dead-end as far as personal satisfaction is concerned. Professor Richard Layard of the London School of Economics runs the Well-Being programme in the Centre for Economic Performance. He has been successful in getting his agenda about happiness and well-being into government policy and on to job titles in government departments, and encouraging the Office for National Statistics to develop proper measures for well-being. Above a certain level, he maintains, rises in income fail to make us happier. We have better health, income, homes, cars, food and holidays than we did 50 years ago, and yet every measure shows that we are less happy. Layard declares that there has been a catastrophic failure to develop a secular morality, and, crucially, that people with religious beliefs tend to be happier.

This realization, that something is profoundly amiss, has led to an explosion of self-help and new spiritualities, and a huge supermarket of possibilities – feng shui, shiatsu, crystals, copper wire, pyramids, t'ai chi,

Gerald went to church to recharge his spiritual batteries.

shamanism, yoga, aromatherapy and much more. It's as if the great rock of the sacred has been shattered into a thousand pieces as people look for something invisible in their lives, without knowing what. But many are well pleased. A woman was quoted in an article in the *Sunday Times* saying affirmatively: 'I have different teachers who help me understand why people act the way they do – my healer Ingrid, my psychic Pauline, and my tarot reader Bridget. What's the difference between them and a priest?'[1]

So people seem to know they need something more, some sort of out-break of spirituality in their lives. The yearning is there, unless it's been completely buried under the concrete of materialism and self-absorption. More's the pity, therefore, that many people don't look to the vast untapped resources of the Church. More and more people describe themselves as 'spiritual' these days, and fewer as 'religious'. Religion gets placed in the corner labelled 'negative, rule-bound, restrictive, uncomfortable, not me'. And yet the riches of the Church's spiritual traditions have sustained civilizations, given rise to acts of spectacular service, and inspired millions to lives of quiet holiness. Why does the government decree that older people should be offered t'ai chi classes on the NHS to promote their physical and mental well-being, but not recommend going to church? The answer is in part an indictment of the Church as it fails to live up to its calling, but there's also an element of a culture rebelling against its parent. One way or another, the Church has to return to offering people the pearl of infinite price – a relationship with the living God.

The riches available

The Christian faith is an Aladdin's cave for those who want to feed and restore the sacred centre of their lives. At every step we trip over another treasure. What follows are simply some of the major 'finds' we could make.

The Bible story

The Bible has proved itself to be the most influential book in the world. It's a book of astonishing diversity but telling a single, comprehensive story about God's love for the world. It's a love story. And within the one big story are hundreds and hundreds of little stories, many of which have shaped nations and cultures. These stories are like the debris from a great explosion; it's the explosion that matters more than the isolated bits of debris, but it all counts. American writer Eugene Peterson captures well the significance of the Bible:

> Reading Scripture constitutes an act of crisis. Day after day, week after week, it brings us into a world that is totally at odds with the species of world that newspaper and television serve up to us on a platter as our daily ration of data for conversation and concern. It is a world where God is active everywhere and always, where God is fiery first

cause and not occasional afterthought, where God cannot be procrastinated, where everything is relative to God and God is not relative to anything. Reading Scripture involves a dizzying reorientation of our assumptions and procedures.[2]

Sacraments

A sacrament is classically described as 'an outward and visible sign of an inward and spiritual grace'. Sacraments take us beyond ourselves into the language of sign, symbol and materiality. Baptism and Holy Communion, in particular, impact our lives with high precision, putting us directly in touch with what's going on beyond our thin words, at the place where God deals with the human heart. Human beings are makers of ritual, and no ritual actions have proved to be as powerful as these sacraments of God's activity, transforming human life.

Worship

We looked earlier at the primary role of worship in the life of the Church, but there are so many varieties of worship in such different styles, languages, cultures and contexts that we almost run for cover, overwhelmed by the diversity. At its best, worship offers a framework within which order and spontaneity can dance together, and draw all humanity on to the dance floor. 'The purpose of [humankind] is to worship God and enjoy him for ever' (Westminster Confession). As part of worship, hymns and songs have taught and inspired millions of Christians over the centuries (Charles Wesley alone wrote over 5,500). They carry our memories and some of our most exalted moments. And if the truth be known, they carry most of our theology too – much of what we believe has come from our hymns.

Spiritualities

Most people tend to assume that Christian spirituality is what they experience in their local church – and that's all there is. They have little perception of the vast array of different ways people apprehend God. For example (and very crudely), Ignatian spirituality approaches God through the imagination, Benedictine spirituality through community, Franciscan spirituality through the emotions, Celtic spirituality through everyday life. The contemplative tradition thirsts for silence, the charismatic tradition for the empowering of God's Spirit, the social justice tradition for compassionate and radical living. The lists of saints and scholars, pastors and poets, reformers and writers, monks and mystics, is simply astonishing, from the days of the apostles and the desert fathers to the sociologists and psychologists of religion in the present day. Christian history is packed with stories to inform, inspire, amuse and discomfort, and after a lifetime's reading we would still just be scratching the surface. If only people knew! If only the Church made it known.

The arts

There is a deep and rich tradition of the Christian Church interacting with artists in painting, music, drama, poetry, architecture, communication and every form of creativity. 'Tell the truth,' said Emily Dickinson, 'but tell it slant.' Churches have been telling it slant for 2,000 years. And the arts are very much the way that many people explore their spirituality today. Many people are reverent as they go round a Rothko exhibition, or listen to a Mahler symphony, or watch *Hamlet* for the fifteenth time. They don't want the clarity and certainty of ecclesiastical words, but rather the ambivalence, the tentativeness, the questioning of art, theatre and poetry. Through the arts they catch the edge of glory, a song in the night, a scent on the wind, a fragment of memory, an invitation. And it's enough. But it might lead on to further journeys.

A history

When we engage with the Church we become part of an epic story of discovery, struggle, failure, renewal and further discovery, as God has taken his people on a pilgrimage of faith. Church history is a fascinating and sometimes frightening narrative, with the spiritual realm operating on the other side of the visible fabric of events. Through Christian history we learn that God has a wonderful way of saying, 'So what shall we make of this?' (whatever mess 'this' is). God never gives up. We learn that God trusts his people much more than seems sensible, so much does he love us. We also learn that studying history is an exercise in humility – we're not as ground-breaking as we thought. Here in Christian history is an extraordinary narrative of God's interaction with his people, full of wonder and tragedy, although the final word for a Christian is always that of hope.

Perhaps this gives just a taste of what could be in store for anyone who decides to take the inner journey seriously and to enter the Aladdin's cave of Christian spirituality. There is, however, one rather important and fearful experience we need to confront – what if, no matter how well we've explored the cave, we don't have any awareness or experience of God? Was it all an illusion?

The absence of God

This experience is much more common than we might think. The saints often wrote about it. Even Mother Teresa once wrote: 'I am told God loves me, and yet the reality of darkness and coldness and emptiness is so great that nothing touches my soul. Did I make a mistake in surrendering blindly?'[3] The much-loved spiritual writer Henri Nouwen wrote: 'The truth is that I don't feel much, if anything, when I pray. There are no warm emotions, bodily sensations, or mental visions . . . The words darkness and dryness seem best to describe my prayer today.'[4] I knew a nun in her 90s who said she had hardly ever experienced Christ, in spite of longing and pleading for such an encounter. If it's like that for the saints and spiritual giants, what hope for the ordinary punter?

When people go to church they may feel guilty for not having any special feelings. Shouldn't there be a spiritual adrenaline rush, a touch of a passing angel, or at least a warm glow in the little finger? It would be easy to feel a failure here and leave the field for an early bath. But consider this:

- Feelings are the least reliable measure to apply to prayer. They vary with the state of our bank balance, our marriage, our indigestion, and whether or not the sun is shining. Feelings go up and down because life circumstances change and human beings are a unity of mind–body–spirit, with our emotions corresponding to our whole-life situation. As in all relationships, what matters is faithful commitment.
- Closeness to God isn't something we can summon up but rather the grounding truth of our lives. We live in God; that's simply the way it is. As spiritual writer Martin Laird says: 'God doesn't know how to be absent. The fact that most of us experience throughout most of our lives a sense of absence or distance from God is the great illusion we are caught up in; it's the human condition.'[5] Most of us live with such a cocktail party chattering away in our heads that we can't even be present to ourselves, let alone notice the gracious presence of our Host. For most of us, normal is noisy. But God is present all the time, closer than our next breath, for the simple reason that he can't avoid it. We may think that God is far away and we have to go and find him, but the truth is that he is right here and we live *in* him. The illusion of absence has to be challenged.
- We may only recognize the experiences that we have already decided will count as 'meeting God', and such experiences have got to be warm and summery. As well as the golden summer there is also such a time as the winter of the heart, the sorrowfulness of human experience, when we might find Jesus tied to a cross or revealed in the pain of the poor. The monk and mystic Thomas Merton said he found a new desert within him, 'a solitude where God is with me [as he] sits in the ruins of my heart'. Not pretty, but real.
- Finally, we need to be aware of what is sometimes called the 'apophatic' way, the way of silence and darkness, the end of words and images and feelings. Prayer then is hunkering down in the darkness and waiting. For some people that leads to 'the dark night of the

soul'. None of this is a choice or a penalty; it's simply the way some people are drawn in their unique spiritual journey. But God is nonetheless closer than we are to ourselves, the ground of our very existence.

All this is far away from the self-help, self-empowering spiritualities available on the supermarket shelves of our culture. But I contend that it's real. This is spirituality in the real world where there are hard issues to face and tough decisions to make, where summer turns to winter, and sometimes all you can do in life is bump along the bottom. The beauty of Christian spirituality is that it has at its heart a Man for all seasons, who can meet us at every point and mediate the love of God.

The God we seek is always so far beyond our understanding it's like asking a toddler to undertake post-doctoral research. But we keep on exploring these mere edges of the Infinite, knowing that this is the greatest of all adventures and the richest of all life's possibilities.

Follow-up for groups and individuals

What experience have you had, directly or through other people, of different spiritualities?

List the human needs that a living spirituality meets, e.g. sense of purpose, contact with the divine.

So what do we mean by 'spirituality'? Is it a fluffy, catch-all word or helpfully inclusive?

What fosters your own spiritual growth most?

What could your local church do to help people's spiritual growth more?

Anchor passage: Colossians 3.1–4.

14

Images of the Church

———➤◦◄———

It is said that there are 96 images of the Church in the Bible. Do feel free to check! The Church is the Body of Christ, the Bride of Christ, the Way, God's building, God's people and so on. Theologians have tried to describe how, historically, we seem to have understood the Church, and the following approach from Catholic theologian Avery Dulles has been widely valued.[1]

The Church as institution

This is the prime way society and the media see the Church. The Church on this understanding is a formal structure, a hierarchical organization with its product to 'sell', its management systems, its employees, its working methods, and its property portfolio. There's a prayer in the Book of Common Prayer that speaks of 'God, whose property is always to have mercy . . .' There's a rumour that there used to be some graffiti in the Church Commissioners' building that said, 'The Church of England, whose mercy is always to have property . . .' Up to a point, the Church does indeed have financial resources, clear tasks and an organizational life, but it only has a formal structure to give shape and sustainability to the inner experience of God and God's call to express and anticipate the kingdom. It functions in the way that marriage functions for love – the former profoundly helps to sustain and guarantee the latter. Marriage provides the outer scaffolding for the transforming experience of love. The Church provides the framework for the transforming experience of God.

The Church as herald

On this understanding of the Church, its prime task is to make known the Good News of God's love in Jesus Christ. It does this in thousands of ways, but essentially the Church is a messenger. Negatively, of course, the Church can then be experienced as a group of people after my religious scalp. However, the Church 'is not ashamed of the gospel' (Romans 1.16) and will keep on enthusing about Christ until the end of time. It's the 'power of God' for both personal meaning and public truth.

The Church as sacrament

We noted earlier that a sacrament is an outward and visible sign of an inward and spiritual grace. So here it would be said that the Church exists to be the physical expression of the invisible reality of Christ in the world. Just as a transformer in an electrical circuit knocks down an electrical current to make it manageable and effective, so the Church 'transforms' or knocks down the overwhelming shock of divine majesty into an experience which can be managed by human beings. The Church is therefore a sacrament or 'outward and visible sign' of Christ. This is theological language but with a very practical outcome: Christ is truly present in his Church.

The Church as servant

Here's an image of the Church with which many people can identify. The Church is there to serve the world in its diverse needs, holding out the compassion of Christ to the vulnerable, whether it be in hunger, illness, despair, loneliness, injustice – indeed wherever people are wounded by life. There's an honourable story to tell here because Christians have always been present in the darkest and most distressing places, being faithful to their Lord. The opposite would be a Church turned in on its own life. After a confirmation in Madras, Bishop Lesslie Newbigin asked the church elders what their church was for. There was a long silence, after which one said, 'It caters for the needs of its members.' 'Then,' said the bishop, 'it should be dissolved immediately.'

The Church as community of disciples

This is a popular image. It emphasizes the corporate dimension of the Church, and that we live with and for each other in this life, and particularly in the Church. 'A single Christian is no Christian,' said the early third-century theologian Tertullian (meaning solitary Christians, not unmarried ones, of course). Communities give us our identity, and the community of Christ teaches us what it means to be a Christian. Together we follow in the new and living way of Christ, loving and serving, laughing and praying, celebrating and weeping: a community of disciples following a life-giving Lord.

These models of the Church have served us well. However, it may be possible to supplement them with some more contemporary images. I shall avoid the suggested image someone put forward of the Church as a game of rugby, where players ignore the ball and simply spend their time tackling each other – even members of their own team, and occasionally members of the crowd. Surely not!

But how about:

The jazz band

A jazz band uses the individual gifts of its members and weaves them into wonderful harmonies. Musicians know the music (the gospel), improvise (adapt it to the context), listen hard to each other (pastoral care), play both blues and ragtime (know how to lament and celebrate) – I'm sure you get the idea.

The carnival

Carnivals are remarkably colourful, diverse events with people's imaginations stretched in all directions. Anyone can join in if they're prepared to throw themselves into it. They want to make life good ('life in all its fullness' said Jesus), and they celebrate human creativity, using plenty of infectious music (and two out of 'wine, women and song'!).

The journeying people

This is one of today's favourites. It takes up the 'community of disciples' image and emphasizes journeying through good times and bad, being clear about the destination but more relaxed about the route, not settling in any one place or culture but being led by a vision of a better way of living together on this crowded planet. Pilgrims journey gladly and hopefully, happy to be on the open road with good friends and heading for a place of great significance – the kingdom of God.

Painting workshop

God has given his Church a wonderful palette of paints, a generous array of brushes and some rough sketches of what he'd like us to produce (the Sermon on the Mount, the parables, his teaching). There's no painting-by-numbers here; God gives us freedom to express ourselves, but he makes himself available as tutor, friend and encourager. Together, the painting workshop might just produce some masterpieces.

Perhaps the Bride of Christ spends rather too long looking at herself in the mirror, but Christians have to see themselves both as they are and as they are called to be, and to recognize the distance between the two. One theologian contrasts the Imperial Church with its mission to conquer cultures and 'compel them to come in', with the Network Church, a mass movement for Jesus embodied in different cultures and built around a network of sister church communities.

Another theologian writes of a *Protective* model of Church which aims to guard the faith until Christ returns, a *Progressive* model of Church which carries on Jesus' ministry of teaching and healing as an extension of what Christians call 'the incarnation', and a *Prophetic* model of Church which acts as a foretaste of Christ's kingdom in the here and now. More accessible images might be: the Church as *nightclub bouncer*, protecting the party; Church as *storyteller*, keeping the story alive in our culture; and Church as *opposition leader*, calling for a different future. Make your choice.

One thing is clear: we all matter, whatever the models and images used. None of us can be a passenger in a merchant navy. A vicar once said to a young woman, 'I haven't seen you at church recently.' 'No,' she replied, 'I've left the church.' 'Why is that?' he asked. 'Because the church doesn't do anything about cruelty to animals,' she replied. The vicar said, 'No, it doesn't – not now that you've left it.' The Church is not that much-abused figure, 'Someone else'. It's us.

Or, as Rowan Williams movingly puts it, 'The Church is the community of those who have been immersed in Jesus' [risen] life, and overwhelmed by it. Those who are baptized have disappeared under the surface of Christ's love and reappeared as different people.'[2]

Together, those 'different people' are the Church.

☆ ── ☆

Follow-up for groups and individuals

What picture of the Church did you have as a child?

What images of the Church (either local or universal) come to mind as you experience it now?

Who is responsible for the Church being like that?

List the ten words that would best describe the church you'd like to belong to. Then in groups of three agree a combined list.

How could your local church become more like that? What could you do personally?

Anchor passages: 1 Corinthians 12; Ephesians 4.1–16; 1 Peter 2.1–10.

☆ ── ☆

15

Mind the gap

———⟫·•·⟪———

I have to admit in the midst of all my encouragement to people to try going to church or keep going to it, that there's still a real danger of disappointment. There's still a potential gap between hope and reality. In this chapter I simply want to warn you to 'mind the gap'. Bishop John V. Taylor took his 20+-year-old son to church one Sunday morning. Afterwards the son said he didn't think he'd be going again. 'Why?' asked his father. 'Well,' he said, 'at one level everything was fine. The vicar said all the right things, but the trouble is he wasn't saying them *to* anybody. He didn't listen to anybody, and it didn't seem to occur to him to do so.'

I fear there's still a chance we may not be blown away by our visits to church. So here are some points to remember.

1   *There's no perfect church.* As the old line goes – if you find the perfect church, don't join it, because you'll ruin it. There's no such thing as a perfect church, because we're all flawed human beings. We bring our own confusions and wounds, and if you multiply those by the number of people in church, you've got quite a potential for disaster. Be gentle with the wounded body of Christ, as you would like the body of Christ to be gentle with you.

2   *Churches are for belonging, not tasting.* As I've argued earlier, you understand the Church and its story best when you look through the stained-glass windows from the inside. From in here you glimpse the glory of faith and you appreciate the depth of the tradition of worship, witness and service. You also meet the strange, motley band of fellow pilgrims God has given you, and you learn

about the movement of God in their lives. And occasionally you find yourself having tea with a saint.

3   *Go and talk to the vicar, priest, minister or pastor.* Introduce yourself and ask for a chat. Tell him or her about your journey so far, your doubts and commitments. See if there is a particular kind of engagement with the church which may be best for you – an introductory or nurture course perhaps, or a form of practical service, one of the services rather than another, and so on. If the vicar or priest is worth his or her salt, this would be a refreshing and important encounter, trying to help you on your journey.

4   *Some seekers and searchers find cathedrals or other large churches good places in which to start.* By their size and relatively impersonal nature, they allow people to play hide and seek with God, giving them space to soak up the presence of God without pressure to sign up for the summer outing or become churchwarden. One of our greatest needs is to provide 'third spaces' (neither church nor home) where people can explore, reflect, observe for a while, and then approach in their own time. Once commitment makes sense, of course, cathedrals can provide wonderfully rich worship and fellowship as well.

5   *Don't tar every church with the same brush.* This church may not be right for you, but that doesn't mean every church is hopeless. I'm not advocating endless church-hopping to find the best deal you can get: that's one of the more tedious aspects of our consumerist culture. Nevertheless, churches have very different characters. One interesting approach was worked out by an anthropologist-theologian named James Hopewell and, using his professional skills of 'participant observation', he constructed a grid of churches based on their dominant character traits.[1] He found that churches tend to have a distinctive 'character', or rather they negotiate between a number of character-types, with one or two usually being dominant. One consequence is that they tend to attract people with similar character-types; they find they 'fit in'. Another consequence is that those who bring a different character to the party tend to stand out as 'radical', 'difficult', or simply 'different'. The character-types he identifies are:

Together, the vicar and the organist chose the hymns for the month.

Gnostic: (Not a brilliant use of this technical word) This type of church moves forward steadily, believing little is accomplished by radical change or unusual beliefs and practices. God's good Spirit can be trusted to bring about progress over time. The natural rhythms of the church's life can be enhanced, but the basic framework continues to be effective. God works through and alongside his people, and much can be achieved, given time. You might just recognize many solid Church of England congregations in this description. There's a sanity and balance here that still achieves much over time to the glory of God.

Canonic: Churches of this 'character' take tradition as their starting point – a tradition resting either on the Bible or on the Church. There is considerable reliance on 'authority' and the church will not move far without being quite clear that either 'the Bible teaches' or 'the Church says' that it's all right to do so. The lines are more clearly drawn in a 'canonic' church. People know where they are and feel pretty comfortable in that context.

Charismatic: Churches of this type are open to change as the Holy Spirit guides. Whom the Spirit guides and what the Spirit is actually saying may be more contentious, but there's a readiness to act in new ways because God is alive, active and expected. The supernatural dimension of life is assumed in a way a gnostic church would find perplexing, and the experiential dimension of faith is assumed in a way a canonic church would find questionable. However, with an openness to the Spirit come risks of interpretation and the possibility of conflict.

Empiric: This type of church is built on the virtues of common sense and pragmatism. Facts are facts, and God is to be found in them. Members of this kind of church are probably happy that other churches and other believers are different, but they are quite clear that the further reaches of charismatic or canonic churches are not for them or (they would beg to suggest) for other rational, open-minded people. Typical phrases heard at a Parochial Church Council would be, 'Let's face facts', 'That sounds a bit far-fetched', and (famously) 'Is it in the budget?'

This typology of churches can be very helpful in coming to understand why you may not have felt 'at home' in one church but you did feel 'in your element' in another. In any particular church people tend to think about issues facing them and their church in ways that are similar to each other, and to be just a little uncomfortable with those who approach issues differently. However, there's great value in having at least some people of different character-type in the church to provide the abrasion and internal critique. They keep the church leadership on its toes, and in a sense represent the views of the wider Church in the midst of the local church.

All this adds up to a plea not to give up on the whole Church because of problems you might have with a particular church. The people of God are gloriously diverse and they gather together in an extraordinary variety of ways.

And if all else fails, remember that God is infinitely bigger than his Church. Keep in touch with the Lord of Life, and in due course some form of church will emerge which is right for you (just about!).

Follow-up for groups and individuals

Recall a first visit to church, or a visit to a different church. What were the feelings you had as you approached, went in, and encountered the worship? What helped and what didn't?

What would you recommend to a church as essential to get right for the newcomer, and how would you do it?

If you have been to different types of churches, do you recognize the 'character-types' as above? What experiences have you had of being 'at home' or 'a fish out of water'?

What sort of church would suit you best? Work out some of the characteristics.

16

My kind of church

There is a danger in looking for 'my kind of church'. It might mean we're simply accepting the 'me-centred' culture which says of everything from clothes to cars: 'It must fit me exactly.' Church then has to be an extension of me rather than an expression of Christ. There is a toxic individualism abroad in our culture which the Church absorbs at its peril.

Nevertheless, the way the Church is embodied in practice is so astonishingly varied it's obvious that some forms of church life will be a better fit than others, and enable us to flourish more fully in love and service of Christ and his people. Within limits, that's not selling out to the culture; it's just part of God's courtesy in taking our needs seriously.

I can think of people for whom silent prayer is agony, and others for whom it's essential to life itself. I think of a young woman who had a starchy Christian upbringing at school, went through a life-giving evangelical transition, and then moved firmly 'up the candle' to a natural home in Anglo-Catholicism. There are Christians who are frustrated beyond words with a formal liturgy, and others for whom it gives order and shape to what would otherwise be the incipient chaos of informal services. I know people who are wonderfully liberated by the life and worship of the Taizé community and others who find it oppressively crowded and overwhelming. Some are drawn to God in the mystery of the Mass, others in the delights of snake handling and leg-lengthening (search the web for details!).

What's going on here? Why do we have such different responses to the same Christ-centred Church and the worship that's integral to it?

Variables

We each find our place on a large Christian map with a considerable number of variables at work. One major influence on what we value and find helpful in terms of faith is our upbringing. What views were held at home? What kind of church, if any, did we experience in those primal and intuitive stages? In any early experience we had of church life or of Christian people, what were the pleasures and what were the deficits?

Another set of influences on our spirituality comes from the nexus of national and local cultures we lived in at formative stages, and the particular cultures of our friendship groups. What did people make of faith, and specific expressions of it? So too our historical setting is important. Being a Christian today involves having different emphases from our forebears in, for example, Celtic Northumbria, pre-Reformation England or Victorian Britain.

Geography too has its contribution to make. Christians worship differently in the Orthodox churches of Holy Russia, the fast-growing churches of South-East Asia, the Pentecostal explosion in South America, the cerebral churches of northern Europe, and the Bible belt in the southern United States. There is no implied judgement in this, simply the recognition that God takes context seriously.

There are other influences: what kind of experience brought us into faith (if that has happened), what kind of Christians were our early mentors, what kind of theology was held by our church, how well has that theology dealt with the traumas that have accompanied us through life? And so on.

But there are two other particular influences that help us to recognize 'my kind of church' when we meet it, and it is to those that I want to turn.

Schools of spirituality

I have found it helpful to adapt a scheme of the nineteenth-century philosopher Friedrich von Hügel who wrote about various schools of spirituality which can, with a little imagination, be associated with particular characters from Christian history. We might recognize our spiritual 'home' in one or more of these very brief descriptions, not so that we are boxed in and bracketed by them, but so that we can be confident in the integrity of our own journey and not be thrown by the enthusiasms of others, many of which, frankly, leave us cold.

School of St Peter

This form of spirituality shares the robust, straightforward, honest characteristics we associate with Jesus' red-blooded friend Peter. If this is your spiritual home, you may well value the structure of liturgy and the shape of the Church's year. Books of prayers and clear guidelines for worship and Christian living are liberating. You'll try to set time aside daily for prayer in some form, and (bless you) you'll come to the events the vicar asks you to. You want to apply common sense to church matters and, above all, you will be loyal; once you've given your commitment you'll be the last one to turn out the lights. Holy Communion may well be your main focus, but more generally you respond to well-prepared and well-led worship. You may be one who depends on the church, but the church also depends on you.

School of St Paul

Paul was the thinker and theologian of the early Church, though he did his theology on the run. He was also a passionate and idealistic man, and could be impatient, having to hold himself in check. If you belong to this school of spirituality you will bring your critical faculties to worship and to sermons; you'll talk to the priest about his or her sermons, and think about how you would have preached better! Prayers, too, shouldn't be too fluffy and over-emotional. After all, there is a real world out there that hurts and cries, and it should be gathered into our worship and prayer. You might be suspicious of emotionalism in worship, but paradoxically you are capable of a deep and passionate response to God, which might make you something of a mystic. Your intelligent form of spirituality comes out of the depths. You can be a critic of sloppiness in church matters, but you can also be fiercely loyal because you care so much.

School of St John

John was one of the disciples closest to Jesus, and tradition has it that he pondered deeply on the three years he spent with Jesus, eventually producing the core of the profound reflections we call St John's Gospel. It's that reflective quality that marks this type of spirituality. It's a spirituality of looking and glimpsing, of waiting and yearning, of exploration and opacity. Prayer needs time and space, and is helped by silence and symbols, imagination and poetry. It's possible that a quiet, early-morning service will suit you more than a mid-morning celebration with all Rabbit's friends and relations. You're likely to be frustrated by superficiality, because worship is attending to the deep, dark mystery of God who cannot be trivialized without paying a high price. You're always reaching out for better things in church, and always wanting the best for God – who is the best.

School of St Francis

Francis is a figure for our time because of his love of nature and care for all created things, including the poor and destitute among God's little people. We probably over-romanticize Francis, whose self-discipline was incredibly tough and realistic, but we take from him a joy in creation and a passionate concern for the needy, expressed in bold acts of sacrifice. If you belong to this school of spirituality, it hurts you when others are hurt, or when there is conflict, and so you'll pray and work diligently for healing, reconciliation and peace. Your inspiration here is the reconciling death and abundant new life of Jesus. You are a doer of good works and not just a thinker. You are the one who visits the sick and listens to the lonely, and sets up the prayer group and the task force on the environment. Every vicar needs a fair few who belong to this school of spirituality, if only because you remind him of the nature of servant ministry and you make up for the pastoral care he thinks he should have been offering himself!

When we go to church, therefore, we will be bringing our own spiritual 'personality' into contact with a church 'personality' which has been shaped by many key people and events over the years. The match may not seem to work. There is value, however, in simply recognizing what is going on, that there is, to some extent, this 'mismatch', and that it's all right. There are other parts of us which can be fed by this worship, and parts of us that we can feed in other ways. There may be much to commend staying in this church and reaping the harvest of wisdom to be found here. Or there may be somewhere else we should go. Either way, God is good.

Stages of faith

The other concept I want to introduce as a significant influence on our recognizing 'my kind of church' is a framework of the stages of faith we might go through on our spiritual journey. Where we are on those stages may well influence whether we feel at home in a particular church or not. The question becomes: 'Does this church express and represent the stage of spiritual journeying at which I've found myself?' If there is too much emotional or cognitive dissonance, we may well have to find somewhere else. On the other hand, be aware that there will probably be people in every church who are where you are, and we could all do with companions on the road.

Work on faith development is associated with the American academic James Fowler, but the typology I use below comes also from work undertaken by Jeff Astley and others for the Church of England Board of Education, which adapts Fowler's scheme for a British audience.[1] They all see the stages of faith as 'filters' which may be placed progressively over the beliefs, feelings, attitudes and ideas of people of faith as they move on in their journey. The *content* of those beliefs will change over time, but so also will the *shape and form* of those beliefs and values, the frame around the painting, if you like. It's this shape and form that the stages of faith refer to.

Stage 0: Foundation/primal faith. Age approximately 0–4

This is a pre-stage of faith where the child is learning to trust by relating primarily to his/her mother. It gives a child its first pre-images of God as the child is loved into being, and into knowing and feeling in response to the world around. The pre-images are mediated through the parents' smile over that most important 45 cms of a child's existence – the distance between two sets of eyes.

Stage 1: Unordered/intuitive faith. Age approximately 3/4–7/8

The child's unordered imagination yields a chaos of powerful images from his experience, the stories he has been told, and his strong imagination. Reality and fantasy exist side by side. Jesus and Father Christmas have equal reality. The lion really might be round the corner. Jesus really might come to tea. Images are more important than stories, and images of God are more likely not to be anthropomorphic, like 'air' or 'sun'.

Stage 2: Ordering faith. Age 6/7–11/12, and some adults

The child is now beginning to develop skills in thinking which enable her to sort out true stories from fantasy ones, and to tame the chaotic world of images. Linear narratives (stories) appear alongside so-called 'objective' knowledge (facts), and storytelling provides an important way of establishing identity. Thinking now is concrete and therefore symbols are somewhat one-dimensional. Moral thinking is based on reciprocal fairness. Note that some adults may remain in this stage of faith, and this will be God's way through to them; there's no value judgement here - each 'stage' is an opening for God's grace and favour.

Stage 3: Conforming faith. Age 11/12–17/18, and many adults

The adolescent or adult here is moving into abstract and reflective thought which is particularly focused on what we are in relation to others. We are highly dependent on the need to conform to what the galaxy of other people around us think and do. We can begin to unify the various influences on us into a comprehensive story, but we are still like fish immersed in water and without the ability to leap out and look down on the water. We are the product of our relationships and roles; in terms of faith, it's not a time for swimming against the tide. Again, this will be appropriate for many adults too.

Stage 4: Choosing faith/either–or faith. Age 17/18 on, or 30s/40s on

We can now no longer tolerate the diversity of roles of the previous stage. We need to know what we believe for ourselves, so we now employ more critical thinking. We are self-directed and explicit, and this can lead to an over-intellectualizing of faith, constantly seeking explanations and meanings. We want a tidy faith, so we collapse paradoxes and tensions. This is often a long and traumatic transition as we leave home emotionally and strike out for autonomy and clarity. And it may happen at any time in adulthood, even to the end.

Stage 5: Balanced/inclusive faith. Rare before 30

Perhaps 7 per cent in the Church might display characteristics of this stage where the tidiness and coherence of stage 4 begins to come unstuck, particularly in the face of suffering, failure and hard knocks. There's a new openness to the viewpoints of others so that paradoxes, tensions and ambiguities are both acceptable and creative. Truth is no longer either–or, and symbols, stories and myths begin to speak again without needing to be explained. 'The self has started to know what it is truly to give to others.' Stage 5 people can be hard for the institutional Church because they're difficult to control. They have their own mind and may want to push the boundaries of traditional, tidy teaching and church practice.

Stage 6: Selfless/universalizing faith. Later life, and very rare

This is the stage of simplicity on the other side of complexity. This is where people have found themselves by losing themselves, examples being Mother Teresa, Dag Hammarskjöld, Dietrich Bonhoeffer. The self is no longer the ultimate reference point, but rather people here are grounded in God and have a new quality of freedom. The circle of their love has enlarged to embrace the whole of humanity. Such faith-pilgrims are not morally perfect but their relinquishing of self often seems to mean that they cannot be long for this world. They quietly go out to transform the world and may die in the attempt.

What is the value of these typologies? Just, I hope, that they enable us to place ourselves in some rough-and-ready way on a larger interpretative map. This in turn may release us from anxiety about who we are, where we are, and how to relate to others on our faith journey. All is well. Let God be God, and let God be God *in us*. If we focus on the risen Christ, he will keep us in a way entirely in keeping with our personality and context, just as, in the resurrection accounts, he met each person at their particular point of need, and held them. It follows that to be at an earlier stage of faith may be God's special gift and calling to someone in adult life because Jesus particularly valued the quality of childlike faith. 'Whoever does not receive the kingdom of God as a little child will never enter it' (Mark 10.15). The basic lesson is to trust God to be alive in us and to take us where he wills. 'The one who calls you is faithful, and he will do this' (1 Thessalonians 5.24).

☆ Follow-up for groups and individuals ☆

Schools of spirituality: which of those schools rang bells for you? Can you spell out a bit more what it's like for you to belong to one (or two) of those schools?

Which schools of spirituality is your local church most like? Do you feel comfortable with that?

Stages of faith: do you recognize those stages in your own journey? What do we learn from that typology?

Is it right to aim specifically to be a stage 5 or stage 6 Christian?

17

Making the most of the service

So we're going to church. What are we going to find when we get there, and how can we get the most out of it? Already that's a questionable question! It isn't 'what we can get out of it' that matters but Who we encounter in it, and that depends on how much we enter into the whole experience. I've already pointed out that we can easily slip into seeing a church service as Christian entertainment. That isn't really our fault. It's the default mode for our leisure-soaked culture that when we go somewhere special we expect to be entertained.

It has to be admitted that if the worship of the average Sunday morning service is put into the same bracket as our sophisticated entertainment industry, it might not come out too well. The temperature of the church breaches health and safety regulations. The choir does its best but it's hardly *Pop Idol*. The lesson reader struggles with some dark corner of the Old Testament and loses on points. The sermon is acceptable but it has no soundbites and there isn't an autocue. At the end of the service you've survived, but you're not really sure what it was all about.

The key is to approach the service in a quite different way. We are here to place ourselves before the majestic, loving Creator of everything there is. It's actually a privilege just to be here. What we are entering is a sacred event which needs our active participation and our eager expectation. Think of it like this:

Before the service

I occasionally wonder if some of us slip into a pew, kneel quietly, count to ten and then get up again, job done. That may be a libel. However, I wonder whether we couldn't develop a greater sense of holy anticipation before the service? As we worship we're theoretically bringing all of ourselves to all God has shown himself to be, so perhaps we could use the time sitting quietly before the service to reflect on the past week, its high and low points, and then, metaphorically, 'take our life in our hands' and place it before God. The attitude we could foster might be what we feel before a concert starts, when the orchestra is in place, they've tuned up, the lights are lowered, the opening applause has died down, the conductor raises his baton, and . . .

Hymns and songs

Music styles in worship are the subject of many books and even more arguments. A composer was once being criticized by a woman for his modern hymns. The woman said: 'I think God deserves our best.' 'Yes, certainly,' he said, 'and that *is* my best.' 'Best' comes in many forms; our task is to enter it and give it our best too. That will mean making a conscious effort to think about the words we're singing. I often come to the last verse of a hymn and realize to my alarm that I haven't taken in a word; I've just been singing a tune (with words attached). Our hymns and songs contain wonderful expressions of Christian truth, great poetry, evocative ideas, exciting promises, deep reassurance – and some dross. But even the dross was written from the heart and deserves to be sung from the heart (and mind, if possible). Of course, if they sing a hymn you know to a tune you don't know, all promises are off; you're entitled to get mad!

Bible readings

It's easy to feel we've entered a thick, dark jungle when we get to the Bible readings, particularly the Old Testament. To make sense of some of the passages we could do with a lot more background knowledge than most of us come with, and some fairly sophisticated tools of interpretation. People talk about 'the plain meaning of the text' but that can often be

They knew it was left over from Harvest Festival, but not what it was, or where...

profoundly elusive. Nevertheless the people who compiled the lectionary of Sunday readings or chose the readings for the sermon course clearly had our welfare at heart, and in any case the sermon is still to come and will hopefully tackle the tricky bits. But let's put first things first: when we listen to the Bible we aren't just hearing a few useful thoughts from ancient literature – we're being dealt with by God. Mahatma Gandhi said: 'You Christians look after a document containing enough dynamite to blow all civilisations to pieces, turn the world upside down, and bring peace to a battle-torn planet. But you treat it as though it is nothing more than a piece of literature.'[1] The trick then is not to disengage the brain as we go through the comforting ritual of sitting down to listen to the readings. Resist the mental temptation to wander off immediately to the afternoon's televised football match, the annoying problem you haven't resolved at work, or the tax form waiting on the kitchen table. Glorious things are being spoken. Active listening is demanding, but it's hugely rewarding.

The sermon

Years of sermons have inoculated some churchgoers against the importance of what is about to take place. This is the time when the *spoken word* is hopefully being faithful to the *written word* in order to lead us to the *living Word*, who is Jesus Christ himself. Unfortunately experience seems to have left many people sceptical about the sermon. I even heard my own wife whisper to our small daughter as I climbed into the pulpit on one occasion: 'All right. You can go to sleep now.' In one diocese I served we had a visitor from Kenya who wrote an article when he left, reflecting on the experience. He wrote:

> I've learned that sermons are to be preached for only ten minutes. Thank God I tried, since in Kenya sermons are preached for almost one hour on average. But in the UK people are very busy and can only stay in church for a specific period of time and the preacher ought to be very careful and sensitive or else you might be left alone in the church pulpit as people will have left to attend to other commitments.[2]

Ouch! As we listen to a sermon it's helpful if we can think of it as a kind of three-way conversation between God, the preacher and ourselves. We listen out for God's personal word to us, we think our questions, we make our resolutions – in other words, we participate in, and even *co-create*, the sermon. We will always be in both agreement and disagreement with a sermon; what matters is what God is saying to us if we'll listen *internally* as well as externally. The preacher is speaking 'in the name of God', and that needs to be taken seriously by both preacher and listener. Preaching looks easier than it actually is, but it remains true that it's easier to *preach* five sermons than it is to *live* one. And living that one is our task.

Prayers

Who knows what goes on in the darkness when eyes are closed and minds set free? The temptation again is for minds to go walkabout. Alternatively we might find ourselves irritated by the sugary tone of voice of the person leading the prayers, or the way he or she tells God what's happening, or the implied political slant, or the choice of things we pray about or don't pray about, or the silence we keep or don't keep, and so on. Almost anything can lead us to switch off in protest or tune out in boredom. Please resist this temptation. The spoken prayers are only jumping-off points for our spirits to reach out to the loving Spirit of God with heartfelt thanks and prayers of need. Try to be truly focused on lifting these people and places right into the heart of God, loving them enough to be serious in your praying. As we do that, we may find ourselves bearing some of the pain alongside those people whose lives have been shattered by the latest atrocity of war or the latest sweep of starvation in Africa, just as we find ourselves emotionally drained when we watch a film that draws us deeply into the tragedy of the plot or the pain of the characters. Prayer is an opportunity to rejoice with those who rejoice and weep with those who weep. How often do we pray to the point of tears? The prayers are not another time for us to be a literary or spiritual critic, judging performance and style. It's a time for deep, personal engagement with the realities of human life, in which we hold together the needs of the world and the endless love of God. It's good if we rise from prayer exhausted!

Holy Communion

In many churches this will be the central focus of the service, whether it's called the Mass, the Eucharist, the Lord's Supper, or the Jesus meal. This is where actions speak louder than words, and receiving bread and wine as a way of receiving Christ's life into ours is an action more powerful than any other in Christian experience. 'Take and eat this in remembrance that Christ died for you' – this is the action that has always most characterized Christians as they gather together. We remember and re-

96

inhabit the death and resurrection of Jesus. We anticipate the heavenly banquet. We receive Christ. It's therefore the most moving part of the service, and we shouldn't skip lightly to take Communion, but rather approach thoughtfully and expectantly. One way of thinking about the act of taking Communion is that when we open our hands, we hold in them all our experiences, problems, relationships, hopes and decisions, and offer them to God's gracious handling. We also bring the emptiness of our hearts so that they can be filled with the life, goodness and energy of Christ. What an exchange – new for old, fullness for emptiness, joy for confusion, life for death. We come away from receiving Communion with full and thankful hearts. We might sometimes, of course, be going up to receive Communion quite at odds with God or with someone else. That's still all right; we're going to receive God's help with the dilemma. God is always the giver. Sometimes, of course, we may feel we're going through the motions, or we may be too aware of the mechanics of getting to the right place in the line, and kneeling down without falling over, and holding the cup without spilling it, to be thinking any 'holy thoughts'. No matter. Remember that it's what God is doing here that matters, not what we may be feeling about it. Christ is the host at this meal and he's the one who's giving his life away. 'Be still, for the presence of the Lord, the Holy One, is here.' If we are not confirmed, it's still absolutely right to go up to receive a blessing. God is always wanting to bless us. And perhaps we might then talk to the priest about confirmation!

Blessing and dismissal

In most churches we are offered God's blessing, his gift of well-being, at the end of the service. It's a final and beautiful act. And then we're sent out to get on with it – the loving and serving and changing the world. As is sometimes said – 'The worship has ended; now the *service* begins.' However, it's worthwhile not to leap up immediately to collar someone you really need to see (or to escape from the person you really want to avoid). We might just want to sit quietly for a moment to reflect on what gifts we have received in the service, the insights, the encouragement, the moments of pleasure. We might pledge to 'take the service home', to take Sunday into Monday and live out our worship in our lives. Then off we go to coffee – and perhaps to talk to someone we don't know.

Not every service we go to will seem to be an epoch-making event, but gradually, I can assure you, we are changed.

☆ *An elderly priest was searching in the wardrobe for his collar before church one Sunday morning. In the back he found a box, inside which were three eggs and about 100 £1 coins. He called his wife and asked her what this was about. She looked a little embarrassed, but admitted having hidden the box there for all of the 30 years of their marriage. She hadn't told him because she didn't want to hurt his feelings. He asked her how the box could have hurt his feelings and she explained that every time during those 30 years when he had delivered a poor sermon she had placed an egg in the box. The priest thought that three poor sermons in 30 years was certainly nothing to be upset about, and asked her about the 100 £1 coins. 'Each time I got a dozen eggs,' she said, 'I sold them to the neighbours for £1.'*

☆ ───────────────────────────────── ☆

Follow-up for groups and individuals

If you go to church, what are your predominant thoughts and feelings as you come to church on Sundays?

Do you manage to think of the words of hymns as you sing them? What are your favourites?

How confusing do you find the readings? What could you do about it?

What makes the sermon a high spot?

Do you manage to pray the prayers? What helps you most?

If you take Communion, what makes that special for you?

How do you 'take the service home'?

☆ ───────────────────────────────── ☆

18

Ten things the Church is not

⬟

We live in a culture which has got over-familiar with the Church. There's a church building on every high street, in every village, on every map. So people imagine they know what it's about and what goes on there. There are quite a number of stereotypes to knock down. The Church is not:

1 *Religious entertainment.* We're all so used to being entertained these days it's hard to keep clear in our minds that the Church is not part of the great entertainment industry. In a culture where even serious matters are reduced to the common currency of entertainment, and where it sometimes seems that we're 'entertaining ourselves to death', church stands out as a place of holy participation. We don't go to church to give the vicar a star rating; we go to engage in the highest activity known to humankind – the worship of God.

2 *Escape capsule* for those who find life too tough. The Church is glad to function like that for those who are wounded and tired, but the call of Jesus is far from an escape to serenity. He came to set the world ablaze with new ideas and demanding commitments. The only escape is from a world of fantasy and dangerous fundamentalisms to a world of reality and the pursuit of justice. John V. Taylor wrote: 'God invites the whole of humanity to share in his exploration of a new world. The Church is simply those members of the expedition who know the One who is leading it.'[1] On the other hand, there is always a place for those who 'are tired and heavy laden' and need to step aside and rest.

3 *Club for religious anoraks.* The Church isn't a club but a universal family. Religion as an *activity* is a place of rituals and meetings for those who like that sort of thing, but Christianity as a way of life is an attempt to follow the new and living way that Jesus has opened up for us. It's a way of holiness, not a way of religiousness. More fundamentally, God isn't interested in whether we're religious; he's interested in whether we're *alive*, and whether our churchgoing is contributing to our being fully alive. If so, God will be in it; if not, he'll leave it to others.

4 *Exclusive society for the super-spiritual.* If it is that, then I shouldn't be there. Those who float six inches above ground and give away their tickets for a Cup Final are very rare, and I'm not one of them. The Church is a family for the occasionally successful who regularly fail. It calls out our vulnerability and points to a man who cried, 'My God, my God, why have you forsaken me?'

5 *Hideout for the Cosmic Tyrant.* Many people suffer from an image of God as the Eternal Traffic Warden waiting to catch you out. Going to church is therefore something like a weekly visit to the police station. In fact the intention of the Church is to be more like the Tardis type of police box which expands your horizons and broadens your vision. The overwhelming concern of the Church is for human flourishing and the fruitfulness of communities.

6 *Spiritual health spa.* Health spas are dedicated to pampering you (I'm told). They'll do anything to lull you into the illusion that you and the well-being of your body are their only concern (rather than your money). Churches, on the other hand, aren't designed to massage our obsession with ourselves but rather to offer a robust, balanced diet of grace and truth. Grace is oil for the soul rather than the body, and truth is a liberating challenge to our mental and spiritual health. But remember: the truth will set you free, but first it may hurt you (said the cheerful aphorism). Truth is undoubtedly costly, but ultimately it's more valuable than being pampered.

7 *Heritage site.* Our churches are national treasures. They cost well over £120 million each year for local congregations to maintain, with

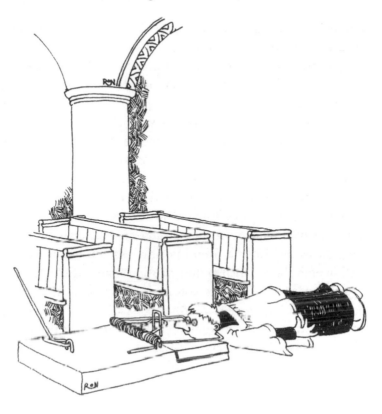

The church mice exacted a terrible revenge.

hardly any State funding, but they contain the story of the nation, and the individual stories of families and communities through centuries of grief and glory. But the churches are not just part of the heritage industry, and the Church's task is to turn those who come through the doors from visitors into pilgrims. One church notice board put it bluntly: 'When you were born, your mother brought you here: when you were married, your partner brought you here; when you die, your friends will bring you here; why not try coming on your own sometimes?'

8 *Spiritual supermarket for lifestyle shoppers.* In a culture where everything has a price and consumption is the god to whom governments

bow down, spirituality is easily reduced to another commodity to be attractively marketed. Large, diamond-encrusted crosses were said a year or two ago to be 'this year's must-have fashion accessory'. All kinds of self-help techniques and fashionable spiritualities are now in the High Street of ideas, waiting to be popped in the shopping basket. However, church is not competing with all this. It's a place where we're shaped into people who are informed in faith and mature in Spirit, not a place where we buy our extras.

9 *Lilliput Lane.* The Church is not a community of nostalgia where the last of the summer wine is consumed liberally and every movement of the Spirit resisted as 'foreign'. Rose Macaulay's heroine in *The Towers of Trebizond* says: 'I am high church, even extreme, but some-what lapsed, which is a sound position as you belong to the best section of the best branch of the Christian Church, but seldom attend its services.' Only perhaps to vote against any innovation. This can't quite be what Jesus had in mind.

10 *The Church is not the Archbishop of Canterbury or the local vicar.* They're only the national and local agents. They're sales, not management.

PART 3

The Church as it might become

19

The Church of the future

Management guru Peter Drucker wrote:

> Every few hundred years in Western history there occurs a sharp trans-
> formation . . . Within a few short decades society rearranges itself – its
> worldview, its basic values, its social and political structure, its arts, its
> key institutions. Fifty years later there is a new world. And the people
> born then cannot even imagine the world in which their grandparents
> lived and into which their own parents were born. We are currently
> living through just such a transformation.[1]

The Church in the past has regularly managed to change to meet the
challenges of a new-born culture. Often the Church has been in the van-
guard as – for example, when the advent of print ushered in a new world.
The gospel has constantly been re-directed to a new address because a
culture has moved house. The current predicament arises, according to
John Drane, 'from the fact that at a time when fewer and fewer people still
find meaning within the culture of modernity, that is the only frame of
reference in which the church knows how to operate'.[2] There is an urgent
task of re-imagining the Church for a new culture, and the work is under
way.

Culture shift

What are the shifts that are taking place before the Church's half-closed
eyes? Here are a few: from friendships based on territory (our street) to
friendships based on networks (work, leisure, college). From a monocul-
tural society to a multicultural society. From a society where people make

commitments to one where people keep their distance and observe. From an economy that manufactures goods to one that consumes them. From a culture of restraint to one of excess. From a core value of gratitude for what's available to one of choice in everything. From families that save to families that buy on credit. And so on. These are not absolutes; they're pointers, signposts, directions. One *Times* reader responded to the invitation to provide a motto for contemporary Britain with this succinct offering: 'Dipso, Fatso, Bingo, Asbo, Tesco'.

For the Church there are some other particular cultural shifts to note. The current climate is therapeutic, not religious; people hunger not for personal salvation but for personal well-being. There is widespread suspicion of institutions because they represent static power-blocks. Similarly, any 'grand narratives' are seen as power-plays. People are happier being tourists rather than pilgrims ('Take a picture, but don't let it interrogate you'). People glimpse rather than gaze; they live in the present rather than in the context of eternity. Theism has given way to scepticism; the prevailing belief of society is doubt. God was the 'locking nut' which held our national life together; now the locking nut has come off, and there's disarray all around.

All in all, it seems as if the Church is in a time of climate change – the whole cultural climate has shifted.

Churchgoing: the state of play

Considering how deeply British society has been shaped by the Christian faith, churchgoing is surprisingly thin. It's estimated by researchers Philip Richter and Leslie Francis[3] that 10 per cent of the population are regular attenders, with a further 10 per cent attending one to three times in a two-month period: 20 per cent, therefore, see churchgoing as a normal part of their life. A further 40 per cent can be called 'de-churched' in that they used to attend but, for some reason, stopped. Half of those might be open to return to church if approached well. The other half have no intention of returning because they were damaged or disillusioned by their previous experience of church. The final 40 per cent of the population are

'non-churched', in that they have never been to church beyond the occasional attendance at a wedding or funeral, and have no particular interest
in doing so; church just isn't on the radar. (In urban areas this figure might
be as high as 80 per cent.)

In many ways the Church hasn't helped itself. Nick Page writes: 'We
built an entire system based on persuading people to come into a big old
building, sit down and listen. It stopped working sometime in the 1950s.'[4]
We kept on serving the same food in the same way and never changed the
menu. We didn't give people the dignity of being able to contribute their
gifts, or the freedom to grow as human beings and as followers of Jesus.
And people grew weary of the Church's petty self-absorption. As Bishop
David Jenkins said: 'Too much absorption in church affairs is a damaging
thing, and total absorption in church affairs is devastating.'[5]

The Church responded to this situation in a number of ways. It said:
'Come to church because we've made it more accessible and friendly',
and this has meant family services, guest services, seeker services, youth
services, more imaginative services at festivals, and so on. Still the
numbers declined. A second strategy was therefore to say: 'We'll meet
you halfway, on neutral territory, where you'll feel safer than at church.'
This has meant services in schools and pubs, barbecues in the high street,
Alpha courses everywhere, special events in parks, night clubs and football stadiums, and so on. But still numbers declined.

What the Church is coming to realize is that what we need is a mixed-
economy Church. The *fringe* might be attracted by better, more creative
and varied worship. Some of the *'de-churched'* might be attracted by
access or nurture courses such as Alpha or Emmaus, and by evangelism
based on relationships rather than proclamation. The *de-churched who
have been damaged* by previous experiences might just be interested in an
apology, and then maybe a new start. The *'non-churched'* might be drawn
into a good experience of community and find faith in the midst of a
church family bound together and energized by faith, love and commitment to Jesus Christ. And scattered throughout this kaleidoscope are the
hundreds of 'fresh expressions' of Church springing up throughout the
land as Christians stretch their imaginations and create new, informal

communities in which faith may be discovered – café-church, church for skateboarders, alternative worship, churches with wonderful names such as Messy Church, Somewhere Else, i-church, Sanctuary, mayBe, Nightshift, hOME, Sanctus 1. It's a wonderful time for experimentation.

Not structures but values

The way ahead for the Church is hugely diverse. The days of Matins and Evensong with Holy Communion once a month are so far in the past as to be a folk memory. However, it would be a brave person who presumed to know what shape the churches of the future would have. It's certain that traditional church, done well, will still have a central place. Such churches, with their visibility, their place in civic society, and their access to hundreds of thousands of lives each year through baptisms, weddings and funerals, are still the ones that grow fastest and most solidly. Imaginative leadership and a warm, earthy, community-related ministry will always attract spiritual searchers and build a strong community of faith. However, George Lings of the Church Army Sheffield Centre notes that mainstream church is now, in fact, a highly specific subculture in society, and it's the edgy churches that are actually trying to be the Church for contemporary mainstream culture. Things have moved on far more than most church people realize.

The Church needs to attend more to values than structures as it looks to the future. The structures have to be aligned with the values rather than the other way around. It's as if we are setting up the loom on which new cloth can be woven by coming generations, according to the patterns which God provides. But since the designer of the loom is the master carpenter from Galilee we can be confident about the fabric that will result – a supple fabric of varied pattern and great beauty. The loom, on this analogy, is made up of the values the Church needs to foster and live by in today's culture. The design of the fabric is yet to be decided. Here, then, are some of the values:

Energizing faith

Conventional, non-demanding faith cuts no ice today. It's an absolute priority to grow and sustain the sacred centre of our lives as Christians and the spiritual life of every church. Without that, there's no fuel in the tank, no wind in the sail, no faith-life to share. Christians will have to be ready to be burned by standing close to the holy fire.

Kingdom theology

Institutional religion will attract none but the pious. A kingdom theology will draw on the teaching of Jesus as he proclaimed the imminent breaking in of a new world. Christians will be reminded that they have to live the values of that new world in the midst of the old one. And that kingdom is an all-embracing, holistic one: 'The Kingdom of God is a healed creation.'[6]

Environmental commitment

No serious person will be able to sit loose to the environmental crisis caused by climate change. Loving our neighbour now is about loving our grandchildren and working for their survival. The future Church will mine the massive resources of theology and faith commitment to lead the new children of Israel out of slavery to carbon, and into the promised land of God's *shalom* with nature.

Christ centred

Jesus makes all the difference. Indeed he *is* the difference. We share much with other faith communities, but our following of Jesus and our growth in Christlikeness is what sets Christians apart as distinctive gifts to a lost global community. We will need what theologian Dietrich Bonhoeffer called 'an uncompromising allegiance to the Sermon on the Mount', and a commitment to following the life–death–life paradigm of Jesus Christ.

Participation

The mood of our culture demands dialogue, not dictation. People won't be told what to think or do. Teams and partnerships will be expected at every level of church life.

Relationships

When it has been in trouble the default position of the Church has often been to renew its structures, but it's the relationships more than the structures that need constant attention and renewal. The Church will have to move from thinking of itself as an institution to thinking of itself as a community, from attempting to control to being content to trust, from living by law to living by respect – or it will end up on the wrong side of history. A loving community will be the best embodiment and interpretation of the gospel.

Mission as normative

Mission will be attractive, messy, holistic and intentional. The watershed was passed in the 1990s when the main outcome of the Decade of Evangelism was a Church committed to mission as a way of life. Mission will have to be motivated not by exclusion ('If you think and act properly, we'll let you in') but by acceptance ('You're welcome to come and see what you make of it'). God is friendly!

Story

The Church's task, more than ever, will be to tell the story, not to create and maintain a system. When Christian faith becomes a system, 'my' system becomes right and 'yours' becomes wrong, and then it becomes more important to stop you getting away with your system than it is to tell the story. We have to return to the noble art of storytelling.

Integrated with life, work and home

There will be a clear emphasis on discipleship and how to follow Jesus in everyday life. Jesus was concerned about making disciples, not making converts or churchgoers (Matthew 28.19). Christians will be a leaven in society, weaving loving relationships, transforming a family or a school, healing, binding up, making connections for the good of all.

Imagination

Church life can be lived at the level of cliché, reflecting back to society what it already thinks about the Church, or at the level of imagination, opening up alternatives and possibilities for human life. The Church will increasingly use the imaginative power of the arts, take risks and sometimes crash, aim high and be wonderfully surprised, make mistakes and learn from them, create liturgies for celebration and lament, be braver, gentler, kinder. We have to learn to trust the imagination as a way to God, and to accept that creativity isn't the same as gimmickry.

Travelling light

The days of heavy-duty Church are numbered. Either that or we sink under the weight of our own structures. The Church will be light on its feet, focused on its Lord and prepared to change direction at short notice. We need a 'low-fat' Church in order to be healthy. We need to re-vision Church as a movement rather than an institution, and one that is primarily committed to supporting lay Christians in living out their faith through the week. This requires a major turn-around in the direction of the Church's thinking and energy. It means that Christians are not seen as serving the Church and its needs, with the Church in the centre of the picture, but rather that Christians are seen in the centre, with everything else of the Church committed to serving their discipleship. It's a tough task, but essential.

Different shapes

I said that these values were the loom on which the new fabric of the Church would be woven, but what pattern will the fabric itself have? In different parts of the book I've offered signs and pointers, and now is the time to gather them up. It's likely that the 'mixed economy' of inherited and innovative ways of embodying the gospel will demonstrate that the Church is a more fluid entity than it has been for centuries. There will probably be a continuing move towards the new forms of monasticism we see in the Northumbria Community, Taizé in France, St Egidio in Rome, and the new religious Orders being shaped by Church Army and Church Mission Society. There will be fewer paid priests and ministers and more 'tent-making' ministries (after St Paul's way of supporting his mission). Already in the Church of England half of ordinations are for unpaid ministry, and projections show that in 2021 unpaid ministers will for the first time outnumber those who are paid. The liberation of the laity is also at hand as every Christian comes into his/her own as a front-line baptized believer. The key task of the Church will be to support and enable these Christians in the thick of mission.

Churches will be more clustered and supported by mixed teams of clergy and laity with particular skills and briefs. Local initiatives will be encouraged, with all the decision-making appropriate in terms of mission priorities, staff, finance and buildings. There will be a growing appetite for celebratory events, festivals like Spring Harvest, New Wine, Greenbelt, Soul Survivor, and great cathedral services. There may well be many Christians for whom such major injections of energy are their chief spiritual fuel-stops and places of belonging. They may sit rather more lightly to local church structures and look for personal spiritual resources in more 'liquid' form – friendships, informal groups, the internet. Pilgrimage is likely to have a growing appeal to spiritual seekers because sacred places increasingly act as magnets in a culture in religious denial.

As the environmental crisis bites even harder, church communities are likely to rediscover the need to tread lightly on the earth, to share gifts and skills, and to monitor their carbon footprint closely. Conventional faith will fade as passionate commitment takes over – nothing less will sustain and energize believers. Christianity will be a movement again, supported by minimal structures, but operating in society in the way Jesus intimated, as a leaven. The Church will operate in both gathered and dispersed mode, but as it scatters it will take the quiet, generative energy of the leaven – and, detail by detail, the world will be changed.

Christians of the future

What of the Christians who will mould the future Church through the use of these values? They will, as ever, be as diverse as humankind, and the usual cast of characters will doubtless appear in the credits. However, here is a particular vision from theologian William Stringfellow who sees the

Christians of the future being 'dynamic and erratic, spontaneous and radical, audacious and immature, committed if not altogether coherent, ecumenically open and often experimental, visible here and there, now and then, but unsettled institutionally. Almost monastic in nature, but most of all enacting a fearful hope for human life in society.'[7] I think we will need the elders and the wise too, but the energy of such Christians is enticing.

I once met a minister from Canada who led one such church. It went like this. The place – Vancouver Island. Dress code – jeans and shaved head. Music – traditional, U2, homegrown. Meets – Sunday nights. Style – informal, honest rather than polished. Core values – orthodoxy, engagement, community, beauty. Congregation – 600 twenty-some-things. It was different, but clearly engaging a new generation.

But, happily, St Paul's Cathedral will still be offering Evensong.

And what sort of spirituality will support us as we move into the future? I think we may well be discovering a spirituality of promised land, of exile, of welcome, of exploration, of being where we are, of prayer as resting in God; a spirituality of fruitfulness, of laughter, of inexhaustible hope; a spirituality of justice and joy and Christlikeness.

I would happily entrust my life to a community of such people.

Follow-up for groups and individuals

What do you think are the key characteristics of the culture we live in today? Do you recognize the contrasts drawn at the beginning of this chapter?

Do you value the 'changelessness' of the Church or should it be moving with the times?

Can you describe any conversations or encounters you have had recently with people in the 40 per cent 'de-churched' or 40 per cent 'non-churched' described above? What can we learn from such encounters?

List the key dos and don'ts for church life and witness in today's culture.

Is your church adapting to those needs?

Anchor passage: Acts 17.16–34. What do we learn from Paul's strategy in Athens

20

Ten things to go to the stake for

———»•«———

I've indicated in this book that not every church is God's gift to the interested newcomer. I've also appealed for mercy on the grounds of common human frailty, and invited the reader to look deeper into the central calling of the Church – being there for God in worship, mission and service. Nevertheless, there are certain features of a church that we might reasonably be looking for; indeed, things to go to the stake for. Here they are.

1 *A church that takes God seriously* – but not solemnly. God is the burning fire at the heart of the Church. The temperature in the middle needs to be as hot as possible because inevitably it cools off as you move away from the centre. God, then, is the joyous companion whose presence is all-pervasive and yet as light as a lover's touch. God is the glorious circle whose centre is everywhere and whose circumference is nowhere (St Augustine). God is the compelling vision that draws and defines the Church, and yet somehow you wouldn't be surprised to bump into him behind a pillar or in the coffee queue. In this kind of church we know that we have been made from love, and it's only in love that we discover who we are. In this kind of church, God is the magnificent obsession who sets us free to sing and serve and pray.

2 *A church that takes our humanity seriously.* Human beings are made of dust, but we're 'dust that dreams'. Add a bit of water to the dust and we become mud, and most of us come to church muddier than we let on. A church needs to assure us of the infinite value of those who

the psalmist says are made 'little lower than the angels', while at the same time recognizing the mud and mess that accumulates around our best attempts to live well. Such a church is welcoming, expansive, encouraging, and extraordinary in its normality. Sunday by Sunday, the walking wounded come in, bearing the scars of the week, and they find there no entry requirements, no exams in righteousness or self-righteousness. Instead, people grow there. They love it. It's home.

3   *A church that takes the world seriously.* We need churches with open doors and people with open minds. *In* with the people of God come the concerns of the world they live in 167 hours a week, and *out* with the people of God goes the love the world craves. Churches are places of compassion and social justice where the dark places of the earth are brought to the table of the Lord to be placed in the light. There on that table all of life is taken up and broken open to the transformation of God, and then we who have participated in the miracle go out to be agents of change, empowered by an unassailable hope that things can be different. This is God's world, for which Christ died, and transforming it is therefore inevitably our core business.

4   *A church that prays.* I was once in South Africa and the service had lasted considerably over two hours already. Lunch was well overdue. But as I was leaving the church with some relief, I saw a mass of women in blue and white settling down for their prayer meeting. It was the Mothers' Union, 'powering up' for their week's work. A church that prays has its priorities absolutely spot-on. Prayer is to us as milk is to a baby, as love is to a newly-wed. It's how we live and thrive. A praying church is relaxed, joyful, purposeful. It doesn't strive. It may agonize but it doesn't worry. It may struggle but it doesn't despair. It's turned towards God like a sunflower towards the sun. There's a saint in every other pew quietly humming with holiness. This is a good place to be in.

5   *A church that sees itself as a learning community.* A learning church is on the move. It isn't satisfied; it knows that the kingdom of God has not arrived in its midst, but that, as in nature, growth is the only sign of life. I once listened at the start of a conference to an African who

Brewing his own Communion wine proved a false economy, Bertram concluded.

had been a bishop since he was 30. Now over 60 and hugely respected all over Africa and beyond, he said he had come to the conference to learn about being a bishop. Such humility becomes us all. If a church thinks it has arrived, that's a sure sign that it's dying. I long ago realized that one of the great joys of ignorance (of which I have huge expanses) is that there's always so much to learn. So it is in a learning church. Its members are committed to deepening their faith, their knowledge, their skills, their spirituality. They're being shaped into the community of God's growing people.

6 *A church with a sense of humour where they laugh a lot – mostly at themselves.* It's very sad when people feel that on entering a church they have to take off their personality and leave it at the door. You catch a glimpse of that when young men, unaccustomed to church and dressed up uncomfortably for a baptism or wedding, are clearly enormously relieved to get outside, where you can almost see them shake off the formality and resume normal living. So laughter in church would be deeply odd to them. But laughter is a gift that belongs to our humanity. It's God-given and one of our greatest

pleasures – as well as being good for our health. Humour should be alongside holiness as the 'ground bass' of our church life. Sometimes as I watch the Church acting out its protocols like vintage Gilbert and Sullivan, I think God must be hooting with laughter (if you'll excuse the anthropomorphism). As if our formalities mattered . . . !

7   *A church where love is all around* – even when it has to be expressed in forgiveness. Love is the litmus test of a church's life. It tells you whether it has got the Jesus gene or not. Love is the projection of God's life into the world and so it is one of the very few things that increases the more you give it away. A doctor once said that he'd been in general practice for 30 years and he'd never found anything as effective as a prescription of love. 'What if it doesn't work?' he was asked. 'Double the dose,' he replied. Churches need to be places where such prescriptions are given out endlessly and inexhaustibly. If people don't experience something different about the quality and character of loving in a Christian community, you can't blame them for not taking their enquiries further. 'God is love, and those who live in love live in God, and God lives in them' (1 John 4.16). That sounds like a cast-iron argument to me.

8   *A church where everybody participates.* There's a town in Nebraska which has only one resident. Elsie Eiler is in her seventies and is the town's registered mayor, clerk, treasurer, librarian and licensee. She collects taxes from herself, grants her own alcohol licence, and single-handedly repairs the town's roads. She says: 'Some day this town will just be memories, but I like it here.' Some churches seem to be heading the same way, because there's only one person who matters – the vicar, or the churchwarden, or the organist. The old do-it-all-yourself, command-and-control model of church life ought to be dead and buried. It is, however, one of the aspects of church life most prone to resurrection. A church worth joining is one where everyone feels they can participate at the level they want – in ministry, in decision-making, in service, or just in quiet prayer in the back pew. Leadership will be dispersed throughout the church's life, although it will have a clear focus in the leadership

team and the one who has been given final responsibility. God is present in the wisdom and gifts of all God's people, and the whole is always greater than the sum of the parts.

9 *A church that looks to the future.* It's important that the Church walks into the future holding on to the thread of tradition. The problem comes when it walks into the future backwards. We need to be looking expectantly to the new generations, the next leaders, the next steps towards realizing the vision God has given. This means particular attention being given to children and young people, and those who have been drawn in towards the edge of the Church's life. Nurturing new disciples isn't an optional extra; it's maintaining an effective maternity ward for the kingdom of God. Key questions are these: Where are young people heard in the church's life? What proportion of the budget goes on children and young people? Is there an adult nurture course running regularly – once or twice a year? How do the church's plethora of contacts turn into active nurturing of those interested in exploring issues of faith? If we're playing hardball, the message is this: grow or die.

10 *A church that knows how to party.* Bishop Jack Nicholls had a simple formula for a successful church – prayer and parties. That takes a lot of beating. I've mentioned prayer above at point 4. But parties are an unlikely tailpiece. And yet, why should they be? Jesus often paints his picture-parables of the end of time in terms of a heavenly party, a banquet where the most unlikely people are sitting at top table, but the food is great (and the speeches short?). Partying together is a subconscious way of echoing this image in the present – as we do, in fact, every week in the Eucharist. Parties say: it's good to be alive, life is for celebrating, and this is a group of people I want to be with. Our local church, believe it or not, is the place where we're given an appetizer for the Banquet at the End of Time. We might as well get in the party mood!

Now, this is a church worth joining! It may not exist, but it's worth trying to create it.

21

So, why go to church?

120 cups from a 200g jar – a personal best and equal to the record!

- Because the people are fascinating.
- Because you might get some rather nice chocolate biscuits.
- Because worship is what we're made for.
- Because there's not much on television on Sunday mornings.
- Because it's good to ask the big questions.
- Because you ought to try out all forms of extreme sport.
- Because seeing is believing.
- Because Jesus is there.

Enjoy.

Notes

Introduction: Why write this book?
1 William Leith, *Independent on Sunday*, 1992.
2 Mary Ann Sieghart, *The Times*, March 2002.

Chapter 1: Reasons for not going to church
1 Antony Flew, *There is a God* (HarperOne, 2007).
2 William Leith, *Independent on Sunday*, 1992
3 Jane Shilling, *The Times*, 2001.

Chapter 2: Why is going to church worth it?
1 Bel Mooney, *Sunday Times*, March 2006.
2 Mike Riddell, *Godzone* (Lion, 1992, p. 91).

Chapter 5: Vicars – all shapes and sizes
1 *Sunday Times*, December 2007.

Chapter 7: 'The cold smell of sacred stone'
1 Jeremy Paxman, Church of England 'Building Faith in Our Future' brochure, 2004
2 Simon Jenkins, *England's Thousand Best Churches* (Penguin Group, 1999, p. xxviii).
3 Jenkins, *England's Thousand Best Churches*, p. xxviii.

Chapter 8: Putting the Church on a larger map
1 <www.adherents.com>.
2 Church of England Research and Statistics Department of the Archbishops' Council.

Chapter 10: Q: What's the Church for? A: Worship
1 Tom Wright, *Simply Christian* (SPCK, 2006, p. 127).

Chapter 11: Q: What's the Church for? A: Mission
1 Simon Jenkins, *The Guardian*, 2 May 2008.

Notes

Chapter 12: Q: What's the Church for? A: Community
1 Geraint Anderson, *Sunday Times*, 2008.
2 Alasdair MacIntyre, *After Virtue* (Duckworth, 1981).
3 Brother Samuel SSF, 'Mission and Community', *Transmission* (Bible Society, spring 1998, p. 11).
4 Robert Warren, *The Healthy Churches Handbook* (Church House Publishing, 2004).

Chapter 13: Q: What's the Church for? A: Restoring the sacred centre
1 *Sunday Times*, 31 August 2003.
2 Eugene Peterson, *Working the Angles* (Eerdmans, 1987, p. 131).
3 Mother Teresa, widely reported in the press, 2007.
4 Henri Nouwen, *Sabbatical Journey* (Crossroad, 1998).
5 Martin Laird, *Into the Silent Land* (Darton, Longman and Todd, 2006, p. 15).

Chapter 14: Images of the Church
1 Avery Dulles, *Models of the Church* (Doubleday, 1987).
2 Rowan Williams, *Tokens of Trust* (Canterbury Press, 2007, p. 112).

Chapter 15: Mind the gap
1 James F. Hopewell, *Congregation* (Fortress/SCM, 1987).

Chapter 16: My kind of church
1 Jeff Astley, *How Faith Grows* (National Society/Church House Publishing, 1991).

Chapter 17: Making the most of the service
1 Mahatma Gandhi, source unknown.
2 Sunderland Minster magazine, 2004.

Chapter 18: Ten things the Church is not
1 John V. Taylor, source unknown.

Chapter 19: The Church of the future
1 Peter Drucker, *Post-Capitalist Society* (Collins Business, 1993, p. 1).
2 John Drane, *Cultural Change and Biblical Faith* (Paternoster, 2000, p. 95).
3 Philip Richter and Leslie Francis, *Gone But Not Forgotten* (Darton, Longman and Todd, 1998).
4 Nick Page, *Church Invisible* (Zondervan, 2004, p. 122).
5 David Jenkins, *The Calling of a Cuckoo* (Continuum, 2002, p. 148).
6 Hans Küng, source unknown.
7 William Stringfellow, *An Ethic for Christians and Other Aliens in a Strange Land* (Word, 1973).